FIELD GUIDE
TO THE
STREET
TREES
OF
NEW YORK
CITY

D1159316

FIELD GUIDE
TO THE
STREET
TREES
OF
NEW YORK
CITY

LESLIE DAY

ILLUSTRATED BY
TRUDY SMOKE

Foreword by Amy Freitag

THE JOHNS HOPKINS UNIVERSITY PRESS
BALTIMORE

© 2011 The Johns Hopkins University Press
All rights reserved. Published 2011
Printed in China on acid-free paper
9 8 7 6 5 4 3 2 1

The Johns Hopkins University Press
2715 North Charles Street
Baltimore, Maryland 21218-4363
www.press.jhu.edu

Library of Congress Cataloging-in-Publication Data

Day, Leslie, 1945–
  Field guide to the street trees of New York City / Leslie Day.
     p. cm.
  Includes bibliographical references and index.
  ISBN-13: 978-1-4214-0151-5 (hardcover : alk. paper)
  ISBN-13: 978-1-4214-0152-2 (pbk. : alk. paper)
  ISBN-10: 1-4214-0151-7 (hardcover : alk. paper)
  ISBN-10: 1-4214-0152-5 (pbk. : alk. paper)
 1. Trees in cities—New York (State)—New York—Guidebooks. 2. Natural
history—New York (State)—New York—Guidebooks. 3. New York (N.Y.)—
Guidebooks. I. Title.
  SB436.D39 2011
  508.747—dc22   2011002626

A catalog record for this book is available from the British Library.

All photographs are by Leslie Day, with the following exceptions: page 35 (*bottom*), courtesy David Bledsoe; page 42, courtesy Nasha Lina; page 113 (*top*), courtesy Zoe Homonoff; page 248 (*bottom*), courtesy Alexander Lein

All watercolor plates © 2011 Trudy Smoke

Maps by Alan Robbins

Special discounts are available for bulk purchases of this book.
For more information, please contact Special Sales at 410-516-6936
or specialsales@press.jhu.edu.

The Johns Hopkins University Press uses environmentally friendly book
materials, including recycled text paper that is composed of at least 30
percent post-consumer waste, whenever possible.

Book design by Kimberly Glyder

FOR OUR MOTHERS, ADELE AND LUCY, WHO HAD GREEN THUMBS

Leslie Day and Trudy Smoke

CONTENTS

NEW YORK CITY, universally known as the Big Apple, naturally prefers that apple to be green. As one of the greatest cities in the world, our vast urban forest also makes it one of the greenest, most valuable environmental assets along the East Coast.

Trees can be found along our streets; in our parks and community gardens; surrounding our schoolyards and playgrounds; in front of our cultural institutions, businesses, and places of worship; and on front- and backyards across the five boroughs. New York City's urban forest is composed of more than 5 million trees and 168 unique species. More than 600,000 of these trees line avenues and streets New Yorkers and millions of visitors pass every day.

In this beautifully illustrated book, Dr. Leslie Day introduces us to New York's street trees and encourages each of us to be thoughtful and caring stewards of our city's urban forest. Her book introduces us to the diverse tree species that exist in New York City, identifies and maps some of the city's most historic and great trees, and provides steps for caring for and protecting street trees. This guide invites readers to grow closer to the trees that cool our streets and sidewalks, help clean our air and water, increase our property values, and encourage neighborhood revitalization.

The New York City Department of Parks and Recreation and the New York Restoration Project—in partnership with hundreds of nonprofit partners and thousands of volunteers—are planting 1 million trees across the city's five boroughs by 2017, including 220,000 new street trees. This public-private partnership will increase our urban forest by an astounding 20%, while achieving many quality-of-life benefits afforded by an expanded urban forest.

Our ambitious citywide tree-planting programs and stewardship initiatives are critical components of our city's long-term health and sustainability. New Yorkers need trees, but more important, our city's trees need us to take care of them so that they can grow strong and healthy for future generations of New Yorkers.

By greening New York City one block at a time, we'll be a million trees richer in 2017. As a result, we'll enjoy all of the health, environmental, and economic benefits trees provide. Using this book, you too can dig in and discover "the street trees of New York City" and help plant, protect, and preserve our city's great and growing urban forest.

Amy Freitag
Executive Director
New York Restoration Project

ACKNOWLEDGMENTS

WHEREVER WE WENT in the five boroughs to observe, photograph, and find our 50 species of trees, we met New Yorkers who cherish their leafy neighbors. We thank you all—you are an inspiration. We wish to specifically acknowledge the following people who have devoted much of their lives to caring for and about the trees of New York City: Nina Bassuk, Adrian Benepe, Sam Bishop, Wayne Cahilly, Elizabeth Ewell and the Greenkeepers, Jennifer Greenfeld, John Kilcullen, Bill Logan, Chelsea Mauldin, David Moore, Karla Osorio-Perez, Barrett Robinson, Judith Stanton, Susan Strazzera, Bruce Tilley, Nancy Wolf, and Christie Van Kehrberg. They made time to meet with us and explain their work and the work and needs of trees, and for that we are so grateful. We also wish to thank Alan Robbins for the borough maps he created to illustrate the neighborhoods of New York City. We thank the following in the Forestry Division of New York City Department of Parks and Recreation for their help: Anne Arrowsmith, Joseph Kocal, Jonathan Pywell, Brandon Schmitt, Matthew Stephens, Maria Trimble, and Laura Wooley. Susan Gooberman, Executive Director, and Cheryl Blaylock, Director of Youth Education of Trees New York, Sam Bishop Sr., President of the New York Street City Tree Consortium, and Katie Ellman, President of Green Shores NYC were helpful and supportive.

For their caring and support, we thank Jim Nishiura, Alan Robbins, Jonah Nishiura, Gina Auletta, David Wohl, Faith Wohl, Nancy Peters, Nancy Leff, Leslie Robbins, Kathy Egan, Beth Weinstein, Naomi Silverman, Jill Benzer, and The Elisabeth Morrow School community, especially Nancy Dorrien, Gil Moreno, Lisa Nicolaou, Al Mule, Jerry Mulligan, David Lowry, Germaine DiPaolo, and Aaron Cooper. We thank the art teachers at the New York Botanic Garden: Wendy Hollender, Laura Vogel, Dick Rauh, Louisa Rawle Tiné, and the students, teachers, and staff of the English Department at Hunter College, especially Cristina Alfar, Harriet Luria, Barbara Webb, Thom Taylor, and Dennis Paoli. Thanks to Andre Barnett, our copyeditor, for making this book read so beautifully. Finally, we thank our funny, brilliant, and supportive editor, Vincent J. Burke, for giving us the opportunity to work together on this project.

Leslie Day and Trudy Smoke

INTRODUCTION

THIS BOOK WAS written for those who want to learn more about their green neighbors—the trees that line the streets of the five boroughs. What species live on the blocks where you live and work? Is there anything you can do to help care for them? Who are some of the people and what are some of the organizations you can call on to help? This book will help you answer these questions and bring you closer to the beautiful world of New York City's street trees.

THE URBAN FOREST

Imagine a place about 300 square miles in size with more than 600,000 trees. Does it sound like a forest? Look out the window. You are in the middle of this forest, an urban forest called New York City. It is a growing forest, with more trees planted every day. This guide will help you identify and enjoy the trees you see every day when you travel through the five boroughs of New York City.

The familiar book title A Tree Grows in Brooklyn downplays the reality. According to the 2006 New York City Tree Census, 142,747 trees grow in Brooklyn, 60,004 in the Bronx, 49,858 in Manhattan, 239,882 in Queens, and 99,639 in Staten Island. Since that survey, some trees have died, but more have been planted, particularly by the New York City Department of Parks and Recreation. Mayor Michael R. Bloomberg has even promised to plant a million new trees by 2017, an initiative descriptively titled MillionTreesNYC (www.milliontreesnyc.org). The initiative is a public-private project launched by the city and the New York Restoration Project, which was founded by singer, actress, and environmental activist Bette Midler. All over our five boroughs, trees are being planted and cared for, improving our physical and emotional well-being.

We New Yorkers need our trees. They beautify the views outside our windows, on our streets, and across our avenues. Trees reduce global warming by absorbing carbon dioxide and solar radiation. They drink up rainwater, which is often in excess in urban areas, and save the city millions of dollars in dealing with storm water runoff. Trees release oxygen into the atmosphere. They absorb other polluting gasses by filtering them through their leaves and stems. Tree surfaces intercept and capture airborne particulates, which are then safely washed to the ground by rain or are carried to the ground when autumn leaves fall. Over the course of a single year in New York City, our trees remove an estimated 1,821 tons of air pollution, reducing the incidents of respiratory disease in neighborhoods with good tree coverage. Trees cool the hot air and provide shade as we walk through the city in summer. On rainy days, we stand beneath them for shelter. Trees lower energy needs of our homes by cooling them in summer and blocking winter winds. One study shows that tree-lined streets have fewer car accidents because drivers slow down to look at trees and because the road appears to be narrower, an optical illusion but one that induces caution.

It is not, however, all take and no give. New York City's trees need us. They thrive when they are cared for, watered, and mulched. In neighborhoods all over the city, individuals, schools, and organizations perform these duties. Several organizations are devoted to educating the public on tree care, such as Brooklyn Botanic Garden, Greenbelt Conservancy, Green Thumb, the New York Botanical Garden, New York Restoration Project, Partnerships for Parks, Queens Botanical Garden, and Trees New York. The city's own Parks Department is the organization we turn to when we need a tree replaced or pruned, a stump removed, a sidewalk repaired because of damage from tree roots, or a dead tree cut down. We have more than 600,000 street trees—and may soon have more than a million—because of these combined, complementary efforts.

A CENTURY-OLD STREET TREE MOVEMENT

A March 28, 1899, article in the *New York Times* reported that the Medical Society of New York County (Manhattan) urged the state legislature to pass a bill that would act "to improve the public health of the City of New York by the cultivation of trees and vegetation in the streets thereof." The Medical Society made the following case for trees:

> It is true that one of the most effective measures for mitigating the intense heat of the summer months, and diminishing the great death rates among the children under 5 years of age, is the cultivation of an adequate number of trees in the streets. Other cities—notably Washington—are cultivating trees in the streets with great success, and thereby improving their conditions as places of residence. New York is without any organized system of planting and cultivating trees in its streets, and, as a consequence few trees are being planted, and the existing trees are gradually being destroyed.

The bill passed and marked the start of the street tree movement in New York City. The legislation extended the jurisdiction of the New York City Department of Parks and Recreation, which had been limited to city parks, to the city's streets. By 1916, the Parks Department realized that, although it was responsible for street trees, it needed to hire an experienced forester to determine which trees were suitable for urban conditions. Trees, chosen for planting by New Yorkers, were dying. The Parks Department reported that "the number of street trees in the residential sections of Manhattan was being reduced each year by several thousands. Furthermore, the department had made no attempt to advise citizens who wanted to plant trees. As a result, in many cases the kind of tree selected was not well adapted to local conditions and shortly died." For the first time, a tree census and tree study were conducted to determine the tree species best suited for city life. More than 100 years later, tree censuses are still conducted every ten years. Through these efforts, we have a better idea about what trees will thrive in the urban environment. In addition, students and adults can take classes on tree care at Trees New York (www.treesNY.org).

By using this book, we hope that all New Yorkers can know the street trees in their neighborhood and beyond. Together, we can value the beauty and benefits of the city's trees. With book in hand, let's step into our urban forest.

1

LEAFY

NEIGHBORHOODS

OF THE FIVE

BOROUGHS

Inspirational things are happening in neighborhoods across the city. Let me share a few stories to highlight some of the many neighborhood efforts to care for our trees.

City Island, The Bronx

City Island is located in Long Island Sound, south of Orchard Beach. It is connected to the eastern shore of the Bronx by the City Island Bridge. The island is 1½ miles long and ½ mile wide. City Island Avenue, its main street, runs the length of the island from the City Island Bridge to the southern end at Belden Point. It is a quaint, leafy neighborhood with lovely little houses, many popular seafood restaurants, marinas, a public library, and mom-and-pop stores. Many residents, like Susan Strazzera, have lived there most of their lives. Susan is known to her neighbors as the "Tree Lady of City Island."

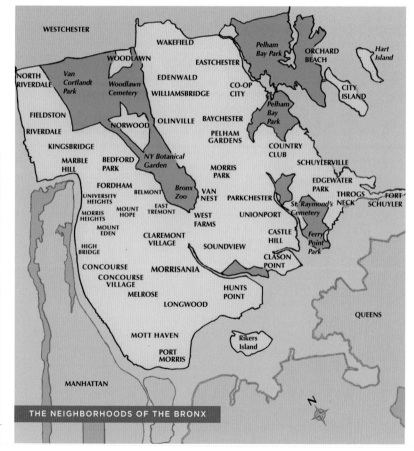

THE NEIGHBORHOODS OF THE BRONX

Some individuals make an enormous difference to the health of a community. Susan is one of them. She got involved in protecting the trees of City Island when the elm trees on City Island Avenue started dying. Through the 1970s, City Island Avenue was covered by a canopy of American elms. One by one these beautiful trees died from Dutch elm disease.

A barren avenue remained and Susan sprang into action. She spoke to a friend who had a business on City Island Avenue and asked her what could be done to replace the trees. Her friend, a member of the City Island Garden Club, asked Susan to join, which she did in 1980. She discovered that the

Susan Strazzera and her sugar maple tree

New York City Department of Parks and Recreation controlled the tree budget, so she contacted them. She wrote letters, made phone calls, and requested trees. Finally, the Parks Department started planting trees on City Island Avenue. Every time Susan saw a spot on a block that needed a tree, she either knocked on the owner's door or called. Sometimes people didn't want trees because they didn't want to clean up the leaf litter in autumn, so she'd wait until they moved or died and then planted trees anyway.

Susan has always loved trees and gardens. Her grandparents were from middle and eastern Europe, and while Susan was a child, they lived in the Throg's Neck section of the Bronx. Her grandmother was an avid gardener, who planted every square inch of land around her little house. Along her driveway she had a latticework filled with delicious grapes. She had a plum tree and a pear tree. With the fruit from her garden, she made her own *lekvar*—a thick Slovakian jam made from ripe fruit. From grandmother to granddaughter to great-granddaughter, a love of growing things has been passed down through the generations. Susan's daughter, Susanna Strazzera, a horticulturist at Wave Hill, a historic public garden and cultural center, is in charge of the annual garden and grows everything from seed.

Thirty years ago, when Susan and her husband were raising their young family on Ditmars Street in City Island, Susan decided to plant a tree in front of their house. "When Mike and I moved in here, we had three little kids and not a lot of money. I didn't know anything about trees or the city's Parks Department. I sent away to Burpees, and they sent me a little tree that looked like a stick. I requested a sugar maple because I love the autumn colors. So we planted it and now it's about 100 feet tall and so beautiful."

In 1991, Susan entered the garden club in the Central Atlantic Garden Clubs' Regional contest for its Environmental Concern Award and won second place. To prepare her submission, she created a "Book of Evidence," which included a history of the trees of City Island, the work the garden club had done to care for the trees, and a complete tree census that members of the club had conducted in 1989, identifying and counting every single tree on the island. As Susan shared the Book of Evidence with me, she pointed out that at that time the garden club had 32 members with 50% participation, meaning that 16 members did the actual work. The tree census was conducted by men and women who knew how to identify trees. "We counted every single tree on the island and identified them," Susan said. "We divided the island up into sections, Team 1, 2, and this is how we did it." Over the years, Susan and the City Island Garden Club have had at least 1,000 trees planted by the Parks Department.

From the introduction to the "Book of Evidence (1990)":

> NEW AND REPLACEMENT TREES FOR CITY ISLAND
>
> Years ago, our main street, City Island Avenue, was beautifully lined with elm trees, which formed an archway of green, providing us with beauty, shade, oxygen and tranquility.
>
> As the years passed, our trees died one by one from Dutch Elm disease. The Garden Cub and community realized the dire need we had for tree replacement. As a result, the Garden Club of City Island has made an all-out effort to replace these trees and even added more trees to enhance our streets. We have worked with the New York City Department of Parks & Recreation and Bronx Community Planning Board No. 10 to have many trees planted and will continue as long as the need arises.
>
> In the past decade, there have been well over 400 trees planted on our Island, and the Garden Club has overseen the well-being of them by having the tree pits cleaned and groomed, informing the residents and businesses of the care of trees, and by making sure that any trees that have been vandalized or have died are repaired or replaced.
>
> We are very proud of our recent Tree Census, which was a mammoth endeavor. The Garden Club was asked by the New York City Department of Parks & Recreation to con-

duct a tree census of every street tree on City Island. The Tree Census rated trees good, fair, poor, dead and where new trees were needed. This enabled the NYC Department of Parks & Recreation to computerize information and they were able to send their work crews to cut down dead trees, prune and plant new trees. New York City Department of Parks & Recreation supplied tee shirts, clip boards, work sheets, tape measures, and tree guides for the tree census. The Garden Club had six teams to conduct the tree census. A total of 200 hours were donated for this project. A total of 758 trees were rated on rate sheets provided by NYC Department of Parks & Recreation.

Our main street, City Island Avenue, is almost completely tree-lined now and our community has greatly benefited from the shade, beauty, and oxygen these trees provide. We are now busily working on getting our side streets planted. We have received many letters of appreciation from residents and businesses for beautification and environmental improvement of City Island.

One thing Trudy and I noticed in City Island is the diversity of tree species. We counted at least 35 species within a couple of blocks. I asked Susan whether she requested different species. "The Parks Department does that because they learned in the past, for instance, with Dutch elm disease, if a species gets a disease they all die," she said. "They try and plant a more diverse group of trees so that more will live."

I asked Susan what she did when people did not want trees? For example, as we identified trees on City Island, an elderly man who was sitting in front of his house said, "Take the tree down. It's making such a mess." Trudy and I understood right away that it was beyond his strength and ability to clear away the seeds that littered his lawn from the gorgeous linden tree in front of his house. "What do you do to help the elderly manage their trees?" I asked Susan. She said that neighbors help neighbors: "We always took care of the lady next door and helped clean in front of her house. We all watch out for each other. The garden club also helps. We identify what trees need. We take care of every single tree. We raised over $12,000 last year from businesses on the island, from residents, from people who live in Manhattan and like coming up here, and we use that money to mulch trees and water trees, maintain public gardens, and place flower boxes along the main avenue."

In the *Island Current*, a local newspaper, a reporter wrote that the garden club's "fundraising efforts provide money for a summer teenage clean-up crew.

This way the club gives jobs to young people and at the same time it cleans up the Avenue. It has seen to it that trees are planted where needed. The club's beautification committee constantly pricks the conscience of resident and business owner to pay attention to sidewalks and yards. It has provided horticultural education to our children and flowers for hospital patients." Within the Book of Evidence are letters of appreciation from former Mayor Ed Koch, former Parks Commissioner Henry Stern, Bronx Community Board No. 10, the Parks Department's Director of Forestry, the City Island Chamber of Commerce, Temple Beth-El of City Island, St. Mary Star of the Sea Church, City Island AARP, Trinity United Methodist Church, and many grateful residents.

Tree-lined street in City Island

Susan believes there are close to 1,000 trees currently growing on City Island that the Garden Club helps care for.

Susan talked about the value of trees. She recalled going to a doctor in a part of the Bronx that was treeless. She spoke of the street being nothing but cement, and how depressing it was. "Don't people realize how important trees are?" After spending an afternoon with Susan in her cozy kitchen, looking out on her backyard filled with trees, bird feeders, and birds, we knew that the "Tree Lady of City Island" had certainly opened the eyes of her neighbors to the beauty and importance of trees.

Brooklyn Heights, Brooklyn

Brooklyn Heights, like most New York City neighborhoods, is a mixture of residences and businesses. It is a green, leafy place because the people and business owners who live and work along the tree-lined streets make sure that their trees are cared for and healthy. There are certain individuals in Brooklyn Heights who devote much of their time and their lives to these trees.

Three of them are Judith Stanton, President of the historic Brooklyn Heights Association (BHA); Nancy Wolf, a tree activist and member of the Brooklyn Heights Association for close to 40 years; and Chelsea Mauldin, Director of the Montague Street Business Improvement District (BID) of Brooklyn Heights.

The BHA was created in 1910 to preserve its beautiful tree-lined streets and historic buildings. In 2010, the association celebrated its centennial. In the 1930s, according to Nancy, the number of street trees in Brooklyn Heights had declined. It wasn't until the 1940s that people started getting involved in planting trees. Back then some individuals worked with BHA to plant trees to beautify the neighborhood. Nancy believes that the Parks Department guided them by giving them mainly London plane trees to plant. Nancy worries about the anthracnose virus, a powdery mildew that attacks these trees every summer. Judy pointed out that every summer leaves fall off, but then, before summer ends, new leaves develop.

The fear that disease will wipe out a tree species is similar to the story I heard in City Island, where mostly American elms lined the main avenue. When Dutch elm disease struck, the street became bare. Nancy is concerned that anthracnose might decimate the London plane population in Brooklyn Heights. Fortunately, as we strolled up Willow Street, we noticed different species of trees other than London plane: maples, oaks, ginkgos, Callery pears, a white mulberry, and Japanese zelkova. There were also many new plantings by MillionTreesNYC. Judy said that the Brooklyn Heights Association takes credit for planting more than 1,000 new trees in 1940 and 1941. For more than 70 years, the residents of this beautiful community have been donating money specifically to buy and plant trees. In the 1970s, the BHA announced that if people donated money for trees, the association would order the trees. For $60, residents could "buy" a tree to be planted in the community, and the Brooklyn Heights Association worked with Kings County Nursery, which is still in business. The nursery truck would arrive with trees stacked up, bare root. Nancy and Judy believe that trees planted with bare roots do much better than trees planted with burlap, and they think the high cost of trees (they mentioned $1,000 today) is due to the labor of covering the roots with soil and burlap. They mentioned Nina Bassuk's research at Cornell University that measured root growth of bare root trees compared with the growth of roots planted with ball and burlap. The result was 200% more root mass on trees planted with bare root compared with ball and burlap. When nurseries deliver bare root trees, their roots are sprayed with *hydrogel* so that they won't become desiccated. Then the roots are covered with a plastic bag. It is easier for volunteers to plant trees with bare roots because these trees are much lighter.

In 2005, the Brooklyn Heights Association wanted to plant new trees and decided, first, to survey the trees that existed in this leafy neighborhood. Doug Still, a New York City Parks Department forester, helped them prepare a tree census. Doug divided Brooklyn Heights into three subdivisions. Volunteers were organized to conduct the tree census. These volunteers were provided with handheld computers paid for by Con Edison, the utility company serving New York City. Forty people showed up that first day. Computers were used to input address, tree species, and tree height data. The Brooklyn Heights Association received permission from the Parks Department to plant trees wherever they wanted to. This was before the city launched its 2005–2006 tree census. Local people continued to identify trees in Brooklyn Heights right through the summer and fall. Nancy Wolf and her daughter surveyed a section and Nancy commented that it was a "ton of work." She was impressed with the neighborhood volunteers who received excellent training by the Parks Department, which involved four evenings of learning how to identify tree species. Nancy said, "There was an enormous interest in trees in this city, not just in Brooklyn Heights, but everywhere."

Trudy and I followed Judy and Nancy to Cranberry Street, which lay sun-dappled beneath a dense canopy of trees. We came upon a stretch of sidewalk where no trees grew and were told that stringent rules govern where trees can and cannot be planted: never directly in front of a building where trucks stop to unload; 7 feet from a fire hydrant; never on a corner or in an intersection; never near a street sign; and never where there are gas, sewer, or water pipes. Sometimes residents want a tree planted in front of their homes, but the city cannot oblige if the location is bad for the tree or the underground pipes that serve the city.

We walked under a canopy of London planes that arched over the street seeking sunlight. As we passed an apartment building with a courtyard and a lofty American elm, Judy and Nancy told us that the elm's roots had interfered with the building's water pipes. When the building's co-op board heard from contractors that the roots were the cause, the board voted to cut down the tree. Brooklyn Heights Association members in the building and along the street were outraged. The co-op board backed down and the tree was saved. "So many people love this tree," Nancy said, "and sometimes you just have to make a stink." She said, "Brooklyn Heights has learned to do two things very well: we vote and we scream and things then are accomplished. That is something they talk about to people who come from stressed neighborhoods or poor neighborhoods. They can do the same thing. You know, it doesn't cost a thing to vote or to scream." She mentioned that there is a lot more citizen activity now in every neighborhood. "But it's interesting that the neighborhoods that almost always have no canopies are the poorer neighborhoods, whose residents usually don't know they have the right to request trees."

Years ago Nancy was part of a group that tried to educate people about their right to request trees from the city. "The organization that I was involved in, the Environmental Action Coalition, which is no longer active, had a little bit of money to do outreach. We went to Community Board 11 in East Harlem, which had three requests for trees that year. We went door to door to talk about trees and asked people if they wanted trees and would they help take care of them. And the very next year there were over 100 requests for trees. Part of the problem is just lack of information. Now of course with Million-TreesNYC, the Parks Department has targeted six New York City neighborhoods in their Trees for Public Health program. These neighborhoods have high rates of asthma and need trees: East Harlem, Manhattan; East New York, Brooklyn; Morrisania, South Bronx; Hunts Point, Central Bronx; Stapleton, Staten Island; and Rockaway, Queens."

Brooklyn Heights has a long history of community activism. It is considered to be the first American suburb. In the early 1800s, shipbuilders and bankers, who worked in Manhattan, built substantial homes along tree-lined streets for their families. In the 1930s, Robert Moses planned to build the Brooklyn-Queens Expressway (BQE) through every neighborhood of Brooklyn. The people of Brooklyn Heights fought back, and Moses instead built a gorgeous esplanade, known as the Brooklyn Heights Promenade, and buried the BQE below that. The residential neighborhood of Brooklyn Heights was saved.

We were now passing Pineapple Street. I love the names of these streets: Willow, Cranberry, Pineapple. On Willow Street between Pineapple and Cranberry, you can see a large, yellow private home. Truman Capote lived in the house when he wrote *Breakfast at Tiffany's* and *In Cold Blood.* There is a London plane in front of 55 Willow Street, and Willow is indeed a densely canopied street. In *A House on the Heights*, Capote wrote,

> For a century or so that is how it must have been: a time of tree-shrouded streets, lanes limp with willow, August gardens brimming with bumblebees and herbaceous scent, of ship horns on the river, sails in the wind, and a country-green meadow sloping down to the harbor, a cow-grazing, butterflied meadow where children sprawled away breezy summer afternoons, where the slap of sleds resounded on December snows.

They said that this house was for sale if I wanted to buy it: for 18 million dollars!

How does the BHA raise money for trees? Judy explained that there are more than 1,000 members. The membership form offers the option of earmarking tax-deductible donations for trees, and the BHA deposits money into its tree fund. The BHA raises a couple of thousand dollars a year for the tree fund, which buys about two trees per year. Last year most of the money

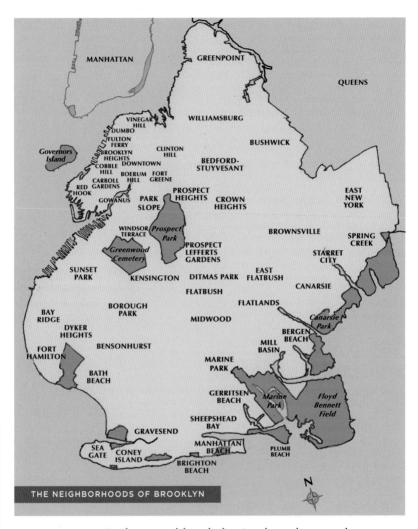

THE NEIGHBORHOODS OF BROOKLYN

was spent on pruning because, although the city plants the trees, there are not enough tree pruners.

Since 2009, Trees New York, has trained citizen pruners, Judy said, "but it is going to take some time before there are enough citizen pruners to go around, and so the BHA pays to have its trees pruned." When Judy sees or hears about a tree that needs pruning and the branch is low enough, she'll contact one of the four citizen pruners that live in Brooklyn Heights to take care of it. Citizen pruners are all volunteers. One pruner asks Judy to accompany him for safety reasons—she protects passersby as a pruned branch falls to the ground.

Tree canopy over Cranberry Street,
Brooklyn Heights

Another contentious issue between the BHA and the city is who waters newly planted trees. A tree care contractor hired by the Parks Department is supposed to water the trees for the first two years after they are planted, but these trucks have rarely been seen in their neighborhood, says Judy. Trudy Smoke and I saw one of these trucks in spring 2009 watering a newly planted linden tree on West 65th Street in Manhattan. According to the operator, the city contracted with his company to water each newly planted tree once a week.

Property owners and apartment residents need to water trees every week for them to thrive. Nancy mentioned that Ithaca, New York, used green Treegator bags to water their trees. When filled with water by residents or tree care people, Treegator bags enable water to drip slowly into the soil around the tree. Nina Bassuk, professor of the Urban Horticulture Program at Cornell University, headed up Ithaca's tree committee, and they routinely filled Treegator bags with water for all young trees. According to Judy, the BHA has ordered Treegator bags for their newly planted trees in the hopes that property owners will follow instructions from the Parks Department and fill them up once a week with water. Nancy remarked that the Parks Department doesn't always tell the property owners to do this and so the bags often sit empty of water.

We were now standing at the intersection of Cranberry and Willow Streets where the trees meet overhead: it is so very green.

As we walk along Cranberry Street and make a right on Henry Street, we approach the beautiful First Unitarian Church. Nancy told me how she and other church members planted trees on the church's block in the 1970s. Nancy stands by the Callery pear she planted almost 40 years ago.

Nancy talked about the large numbers of trees counted in the "brownstone" neighborhoods of Brooklyn Heights that form a dense canopy. She said that although the "transitional" blocks of Brooklyn Heights, the blocks that were between the residential blocks and the blocks of downtown Brooklyn, had

Open trench tree pit with Belgian blocks

fewer trees, more were being planted. "Now," she said, "they are planting trees like mad" on the transitional blocks and in downtown Brooklyn. What makes these trees have a better chance of survival is that the business improvement districts and community boards are using "open trench"–style tree pits.

Nina Bassuk invented this method of planting trees so that there would be more open soil to collect rainwater and oxygen. The transitional block of Pierrepont Street between Clinton Street and Cadman Plaza in the 1980s was the site of a battle between the neighborhood and the developer of a high-rise office tower. In the end, the developer let the citizens of Brooklyn Heights decide on the type of trees to be planted and, as requested, nonreflective windows were used to reduce glare. The landscape architect for the building wanted to plant Japanese zelkova trees on two of the blocks along the building, but Nancy pointed out that one side was in full sun and one side was in shade. She made a case for more diverse species. The developer gave them what they wanted. They brought in forester Bill Lough from the Parks Department and Nina Bassuk from Cornell University to design the open trenches and choose appropriate species of trees for the site. Red maples were planted on one side, and pin oaks on the other. Between the Belgian blocks (see figure), soil is visible. This design, of long trenches with open areas of soil between the blocks, keeps the soil from compacting and allows rainwater and oxygen to enter.

Moving from the "transitional" blocks to the busy business district of Montague Street, we meet Chelsea Mauldin, Director of the Montague Street Business Improvement District in Brooklyn Heights.

According to Chelsea, money collected from properties in the Montague Street BID is used for the tree-lined blocks of quaint Montague Street. Chelsea has also obtained city funding and worked with the Parks Department to install new tree guards around the tree pits to protect existing trees. To do that, they had to know the number of trees, so they conducted a census to identify tree species. They didn't want some of the pits to be as big as others, because some merchants have sidewalk cafes or other sidewalk activities. Wide pits would narrow the sidewalk. The Parks Department accommodated the BID's requests. One Brooklyn forester was happy to look at each pit, one by one. Chelsea asked her to identify trees because she didn't know their names and wanted to make a survey of the species. That led Chelsea to create a list of all the trees on Montague Street. Chelsea's understanding is that there is not a surprising selection of street trees along Montague Street: ginkgos, lindens, and Callery pears, the usual suspects. They look well loved and cared for. Chelsea has also established an ongoing relationship with the arborist Bill Logan, who comes out to Montague Street once a year. Bill also trains arborists in the Parks Department. According to Chelsea, "he speaks 'tree language' and

Montague Street Business Improvement District banner

lets us know what the trees need and prunes them and adds soil amendments. He saws off dead branches before they fall down and generally takes care of the trees." We walked along Montague Street past St. Ann and the Holy Trinity Church.

"These trees are such a great asset in a commercial district," Chelsea said. "They create a wonderful feeling on the street for businesses. They make the street beautiful, and it's well worth it for the businesses to donate money and invest in the health and care of these trees."

I asked Chelsea where the BID gets its money. Every BID throughout the five boroughs is written into law, she said. Each BID is created by local and state legislation. It becomes a special taxation district: each property within the district is assessed a mandatory fee. In the Montague district, the fee is half based on the assessed value of the building and half on the length of the street frontage of the building. The owner of a tall, wide building pays more than the owner of a smaller building. The annual budget for the district is $175,000, and the budget is apportioned among all properties in the district based on that formula. BIDs exist only where the local communities have decided to establish them. At present, there are more than 60 across the five boroughs. All but two or three are commercial BIDs. A couple are industrial BIDs, including an industrial BID in East New York. BIDs were created to improve businesses, the business community, and neighborhoods. BIDs are not residential.

When a BID is under consideration, community meetings are held. Before legislation can move forward, an official poll is taken and at least 50% of the property owners in the proposed district cannot be opposed. As Chelsea explained, "It's constituted as a not-for-profit district management association, a 501(c)(3), which is the organization that I'm the director of. I have a board of directors that are broken into five categories; property owners, commercial tenants, residential tenants, representatives from the local community board, and from the residential Brooklyn Heights Association, and we meet quarterly, and one of those meetings is an annual meeting.

"Creating a BID is voluntary, but once it's instituted it is no longer voluntary. Each BID is its own incorporated not-for-profit entity in partnership with the New York City Department of Small Business Services. The city collects the assessments on our behalf through taxes and then hands the money to us. We have a contract with the city to do that service. The first BID got started about 25 years ago. This Brooklyn Heights BID was created about 13 years ago. Mayor Bloomberg has been in favor of them so the number of BIDs has doubled during his terms as mayor. The very first BID was created in Toronto about 30 years ago. This was a Canadian idea that has taken hold in New York City."

Chelsea, her husband, software developer Adam Young, and their two young sons live in nearby Carroll Gardens, Brooklyn. Chelsea bicycles to her office in St. Ann's church and works hard to keep Montague Street green and healthy.

Hamilton Heights, West Harlem, Manhattan

Bruce Tilley is a member of the Hamilton Terrace Block Association and the Hamilton Heights Homeowners Association. We met in early August, and Bruce took me on a tour of his beautiful and historic neighborhood.

Bruce has been trying to help the community with its trees. "Most people love the trees," he said. This spring Bruce petitioned the Parks Department and received "a truckload of wood chips, so we could mulch all the tree pits. Quite a few children and adults came out to help. Parks dumped the wood chips in a parking spot in the middle of the block. We carried it in garbage pails and covered all the tree pits." As we walked south on Hamilton Terrace toward West 141st Street, I noticed a large wooden mansion on grounds just south of City College. Bruce told me that it was Alexander Hamilton's home, called the

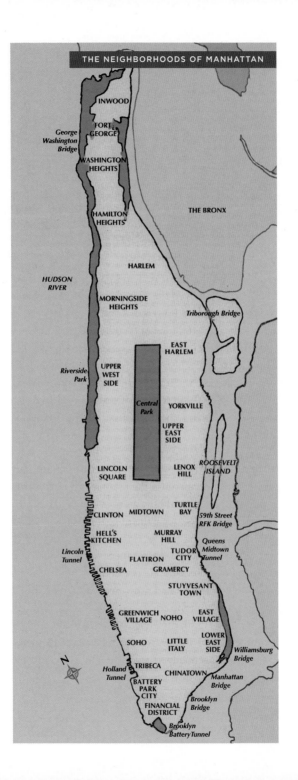

THE NEIGHBORHOODS OF MANHATTAN

INWOOD

FORT GEORGE

George Washington Bridge

WASHINGTON HEIGHTS

HAMILTON HEIGHTS

THE BRONX

HARLEM

HUDSON RIVER

MORNINGSIDE HEIGHTS

Triborough Bridge

EAST HARLEM

Riverside Park

UPPER WEST SIDE

Central Park

YORKVILLE

UPPER EAST SIDE

LINCOLN SQUARE

LENOX HILL

ROOSEVELT ISLAND

TURTLE BAY

CLINTON   MIDTOWN

59th Street RFK Bridge

HELL'S KITCHEN

MURRAY HILL

Queens Midtown Tunnel

Lincoln Tunnel

FLATIRON

TUDOR CITY

CHELSEA

GRAMERCY

STUYVESANT TOWN

GREENWICH VILLAGE   NOHO

EAST VILLAGE

SOHO

LITTLE ITALY

LOWER EAST SIDE

Williamsburg Bridge

Holland Tunnel

TRIBECA

CHINATOWN

Manhattan Bridge

BATTERY PARK CITY

Brooklyn Bridge

FINANCIAL DISTRICT

Brooklyn Battery Tunnel

N

LEAFY NEIGHBORHOODS OF THE FIVE BOROUGHS | 33

Tree canopy over Convent Avenue, West Harlem

Hamilton Grange, a National Historic Landmark. Bruce told the story of how the National Park Service moved the Hamilton Grange from where it had sat for years next to the St. Luke's Episcopal Church on Convent Avenue, down West 141st Street to its present home in St. Nicholas Park at Hamilton Terrace and 141st Street. "When they moved the home," Bruce said, "we lost about 14 mature trees along 141st Street because they made the street level by rebuilding the incline with dirt so that the house would not have to move down such a steep hill." After removing those trees, Bruce advocated for tree replacement, and today many new trees have been planted in large tree pits. Bruce's next move is to mulch these.

As we walked up Convent Avenue, I asked Bruce whether anyone filled the Treegator bags around the newly planted trees. He said that the National Park Service, stationed there because the Grange is a national monument, fill the Treegator bags. He mentioned how great it was to have both the National Park Service and the city Parks Department to turn to for help with trees. "We are trying to capitalize on the preparation of the opening of the Alexander Hamilton National Monument—the Grange—to help push a beautification aspect for our community," he said. He pointed to a newly planted tree. "That tree was replaced because the pit had been empty for years. We are now in the process of forming a tree committee."

Bruce tells me that Hamilton Heights was developed in the late 1800s as a community of summer homes for wealthy merchant families from the Lower East Side. There are many synagogues, churches, and mosques in the neighborhood. "The history of the neighborhood is all turn of the century," he said. "There are many mature trees because the neighborhood is more than 100 years old." Overhead is a green canopy that completely shades Convent Avenue.

Trees taking over abandoned school building, P.S. 186, on West 145th Street, Harlem

We walk to West 145th Street, west of Amsterdam Avenue so that Bruce can show me an abandoned school building, P.S. 186, which was given to the

Neighbors working together, building a wooden tree guard on West 144th Street, Harlem

Boys and Girls Club of Harlem in 1986. The school's windows and roof are gone. Nothing has been done to rebuild or renovate the structure since the mid-1970s, and when I look up I am completely astonished to see that trees have taken over the building. They are growing out of every window and through the roof. I identify paulownia, mulberry, cottonwood, maple, and ailanthus trees. What a site! People of the neighborhood are fighting to preserve and restore the beautiful 108-year-old Italianate school structure.

We finished up our tour with a visit to West 144th Street between Amsterdam Avenue and Broadway. On May 15, 2010, the West 144th Street Block Association had a block beautification day, in which residents, young and old, cleaned graffiti, planted flowers, mulched tree pits, and built tree guards. The motto that inspired the beautification day: "Less Rats, More Trees!"

Upper West Side, Manhattan

About 3 miles south of Hamilton Heights is the Upper West Side. During the scorching, hot summer of 2010, as I worked on this book with Trudy Smoke, she saw some men watering trees on Broadway and noticed the word "Greenkeepers" on their t-shirts. She found out that they were part of the

Goddard-Riverside Community Center on Manhattan's Upper West Side. I contacted them and arranged to meet with a coordinator of this amazing program.

Elizabeth Ewell is the business manager for Greenkeepers, an organization that trains formerly homeless men and women in horticulture and tree care.

Elizabeth and I sat in a garden behind Goddard-Riverside's Phelps House, a large apartment complex housing senior citizens on Columbus Avenue between 88th and 89th Streets. Goddard-Riverside was formed in 1959 when two settlement houses merged. Riverside Community House and Goddard Neighborhood Center were founded in the late nineteenth century during the height of the "settlement" movement, when social workers "settled," or lived in poor neighborhoods to understand the problems and create services within the neighborhoods to solve those problems.

The Phelps House garden is a place for putterers: residents who love to plant and weed. A greenhouse can be used during winter. Arthur, a staff member, keeps the garden in beautiful condition. We sat in the garden on a hot, steamy August day, but in the shade of the trees and shrubs, the air felt comfortable. In a nearby tree, a male cardinal sang. It was relaxing and peaceful .

Elizabeth explained the history and mission of Greenkeepers: "Greenkeepers is approximately 15 years old. Our mission is to employ adults living with mental illness. These are people that were previously homeless and have come through the outreach and treatment process. Now they are stable and they are looking for employment. Some haven't worked in years, and others have never worked. So they come to TOP Opportunities. TOP stands for The Other Place, a program set up to help people reenter or enter the workforce. Employment specialists work with the clients to help them develop their skills or polish their job skills, go through the whole job search process, find them interviews, take them to the interviews, and offer support during the process. Greenkeepers is what's called 'supported employment.' We are the employer, and we have employment specialists that I work very closely with. We support our men and women. If they have appointments, I make allowances if they are late. I make allowances if they forget they had an appointment or if they forgot to tell me at the last minute. They get on-the-job training. If you are a person who is entering the workforce and you're not in the habit of getting up early, being on time, scheduling your time properly so that you can get to work, the employment specialist helps you get the job skills and the life skills that you need. The employment specialists work for the Goddard-Riverside TOP Opportunities program. They are the ones that work closely with each client to make sure that they keep a job once they get one. It's one thing to place a person in a job, but if you don't support them, they won't be successful.

"Our mission as Greenkeepers is to help people living with mental illness who were previously homeless. They come in under TOP; they interview to get into TOP and have to be referred. They have to want a job, and they have to want to work with a job preparation program. During the interview, I ask them if they've worked with plants before and what interests them in working with plants. I ask them if they understand that it's hard work, not easy work. Are they willing to get dirty? I tell them that there's a lot of heat out there and is that going to bother them? And they almost immediately become a Greenkeeper. They train for eight sessions. It's on-the-job training, so it's eight assignments, three or four times a week out in the field before they become employees and go on payroll, starting at minimum wage. That's just the initial training. For Greenkeepers, training is ongoing. Those sessions are to help get them into the habit of being on time and getting their uniform, making sure they come prepared. We supply their uniforms: a green t-shirt with the Greenkeepers name on it, the Greenkeepers hat, and standard green work pants. They have to buy their own work boots. If they don't have money to buy boots, we work with them and help them save from their stipend pay from their training and their first paycheck. We started out in 1995 working with the Lincoln Square Business Improvement District and Broadway Malls."

Broadway Malls are the medians in the middle of Broadway planted with beautiful flowers and mature trees. Broadway Malls run from 70th Street to 168th Street. Elizabeth said that when they started working on the Broadway Malls, the malls did not look like they do today. "We have worked with the Broadway Malls organization from West 86th Street to 96th Street almost from the beginning," she said. "We plant flowers there. We prune and care for the trees there." Greenkeepers uses the citizen pruner course given by Trees New York. Greenkeepers also has an experienced horticulturist on staff named Leslie Ware. When I asked Elizabeth whether Greenkeepers worked in Riverside Park she told me that they usually work with the Riverside Park Fund volunteer, David Goldstick, helping him with his extensive garden that runs from 79th Street to 83rd Street along the West Side Highway within the park. I told her that he is one of my favorite people. David, known as "the garden man," is a retired real estate attorney who has spent decades beautifying Riverside Park by planting thousands of flowers, trees, and shrubs, such as the gorgeous crape myrtle that blooms throughout the summer. I had brought some of my students from our nature photography club to Riverside Park in May to photograph the plants and the red-tailed hawk nest near the 79th Street Boat Basin,

Greenkeepers' watering machines

and we encountered David and a group of men working with him. Now I know that those men were Greenkeepers.

Elizabeth said that her Greenkeepers work with the Broadway BIDs from 70th Street to 168th Street. They do horticulture mainly between 86th and 96th Streets and sanitation and watering throughout the rest of the malls. They pick up garbage, sweep, and water the trees in the malls. As I listen to the taped interview, I hear myself saying, "Thank you, thank you, thank you." I was born on West 73rd Street and have lived on the Upper West Side most of my life and not a day goes by without my thinking about the beauty of this neighborhood. The Broadway Malls have greatly added to that beauty, with interesting gardens, trellises, and trees. The Greenkeepers can take a lot of credit for this. Three days a week they are on Broadway from 86th to 96th streets, pruning trees and caring for plants. They are equipped with the tools of citizen pruners: pole saws, clippers, and loppers. They have a watering machine on wheels that holds 40 gallons of water.

I asked Elizabeth if they were watering tree pits during the terrible summer drought and heat wave. "My guys were out watering tree pits today on West 77th Street between Columbus and Central Park West. At the beginning of the season, arrangements are made with a building superintendent or building owner in the assigned areas to provide us with water. They use watering machines and carry hoses in case they can hook up to a spigot on the outside of a building.

"Block associations hire us to maintain their trees. This can include anything from soil preparation for them to do their annual spring planting, to watering the flowers, which is really watering the trees. When we clean out the tree pits, we'll put in mulch if we're asked to, which keeps the tree pits healthy and makes them look good. That's half the problem right there: people ignore the tree pits until they look absolutely horrendous and at that point we have almost cement-like dirt. Another area we've been working on for years is East 86th Street from Lexington Avenue to First Avenue. We started over there with just digging out and replacing the soil in the tree pits the first few years. The East 86th Street Merchants and Residents Association hires us."

Elizabeth tells me that Greenkeepers' clients include "building owners, block associations, and BIDs. I go out to drum up business by giving my three-minute spiel at community board meetings and street fairs to get the word out about what we do. Work has gradually picked up. During the season, we have a good amount of work every day. The more work we get, the more people I can hire from a special needs population. I'm always looking to grow work for us to make sure that we have enough work so a person can see a decent paycheck. I want to be able to expand and hire more people from the different special needs programs. Once someone is interested in hiring us, I go and look at the job and we do an assessment on how much it will cost. When we get a job to plant flowers in tree pits, we have vendors throughout the city that supply the flowers. One is the Brooklyn Terminal Market. A lot of our customers, like block associations, will have their annual spring planting day, when volunteers come out and plant, but we'll do the advance work for them. We'll clean up the tree pits, prepare the dirt, add fertilizer to the soil, get it ready for the flowers to be planted."

As the Greenkeepers help the trees of the Upper West Side, the trees help them.

Astoria, Queens

In Astoria, Queens, a hardy group of women and men care for neighborhood trees and parks. They are known as Green Shores NYC. Christie Van Kehrberg, semiretired, is head of Green Shores' street tree committee. On a scorching hot day in late July, Trudy and I went to her lovely prewar apartment in Astoria and interviewed her about her work with Astoria's street trees. As soon as we arrived, she offered homemade iced green tea, and as I wandered toward her living room, I noticed a green hose curled up in her bathtub. Living on a boat, I am used to seeing all kinds of hoses in all kinds of places, but it is rare to see a hose in a New York City apartment bathtub. I asked her whether she used that particular hose to water trees on the street. She did. "But," she said, "I don't always have access to a spigot and so I water using 12 three-liter jugs that I transport in my market cart." Christie said that a physical therapy office lets her fill up her bottles in their kitchen. "I have about 16 trees that I try to water every week. If they have Treegators, I can almost fill one bag. I have 12 bottles, holding about 10 gallons of water, that's 75 pounds of water that I'm pushing around. I go down to my laundry room and fill up. If there's not a gator bag on the tree, it depends on whether there's any kind of mulch as to how much water I can put into the tree bed and not just have it run out onto

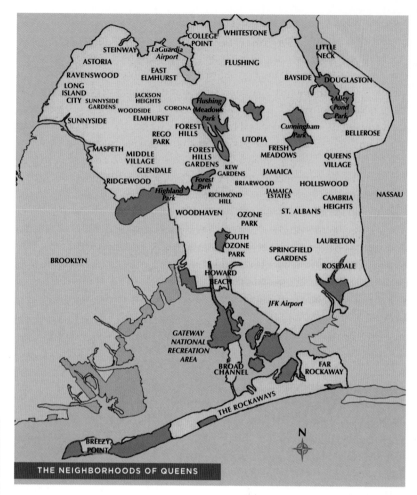

THE NEIGHBORHOODS OF QUEENS

the street. I might be able to dump two of them in, or four at the absolute most.
I can rotate some of the Treegators. They are hard to get off, but there are zip-
pers. You can zip them off and put them on another tree. It's a lot of work, but
it's been so dry! We had that period with seven weeks of no rain in Astoria, and
100-degree days. Then we had kind of a flash flood. Now we've had a few more
weeks of no rain. The trees on my street are of varying ages. This is the third
year that some of them are in, but I've got bags for them, and I'm still watering
them. Then there are some that are in for four or five years, but they are not
well established, so I water them. There are other trees that I know from the
tags that this is their second season, so I care for them. I take care of various
trees two blocks in each direction."

When asked about the history of Green Shores and how the street tree committee came to be, Christie said, "Well, I discovered Green Shores after I became a citizen pruner in the spring of 2008. I had gone to a talk at the New York Horticultural Society and Alex Feleppa, who was their director of horticulture, mentioned Treegators that the Parks Department was putting around street trees. And that although a subcontractor was supposed to fill those bags once a week, it really wasn't enough water. I said that I had four new trees on my block with those gator bags and that I would volunteer to fill them. Then Alex said, 'Well, why don't you become a citizen pruner,' which I followed through on. I wasn't really familiar with the parks groups in my area because I had been working full time up until then. I was looking around for a parks group to work with and was led to Green Shores. I was looking for other citizen pruners and they asked me to organize a street tree committee. It turned out that some of the people in the group were already citizen pruners, but they had no tools, they had never been out and were too shy to go out on their own.

"Other people had taken a course with Partnerships for Parks: An Evening of Stewardship, so they felt this was something they should do, but it just hadn't gotten itself organized, so I set a date and waited to see who would show up. I already had tools: a pole saw, a folding hand saw, a hand rake and mallet to loosen heavily compacted soil. It has a sharp edge so if you angle it as you strike, you can break up that top edge of hard soil and still avoid breaking the roots. They went over all of these tools with us in the citizen pruner class. It's a twelve-hour class consisting of four sessions, one of which is working out on the street. You actually handle the tools and then you buy your own. If you take one of the evening classes with Partnerships for Parks or now with Million-TreesNYC, they will give you a hoe, a bucket, gloves, and a weeder. Otherwise, citizen pruners have to buy their own tools."

In her search for other citizen pruners, Christie learned about the Gantry Park people and found them to be a very well established group of volunteers. "They go out once a month as a group and I go with them. Some of them have been doing this for ten years. I learn a lot when I go out with them. They are very thoughtful. When they look at a tree they talk about what they think should be done. They don't just rush in and start hacking away. And they are cognizant of what a tree needs. If a tree is very stressed they'll pass it by. Any kind of cut that you make traumatizes the tree. If vandals have cut into the tree it has to recover from that. So if the tree is already struggling, you should just leave it alone. Call 311 and let the professionals work with it. There are plenty of other things we can do: water it, loosen the soil in the tree pit." It reminded me of when humans have a surgical procedure and that we need to be as strong and healthy as possible leading up to surgery.

The Gantry Park volunteers work with trees within Gantry Park and along the streets around the park. With the forester's permission, you can prune in a park, but citizen pruners are confined to the streets. A citizen pruner can work on any tree on the street, but permission is needed to prune in the park from whomever is in charge of the park. I asked Christie what other groups compose Green Shores NYC. She brought out a beautiful map of the Green Shores area, which includes Ralph DeMarco Park, Astoria Park, Whitey Ford Park, Socrates Sculpture Park, Two Coves Community Garden, Queensbridge Park, and Rainey Park.

Green Shores NYC volunteers carting pruned tree limbs on a bicycle to a park nearby for chipping

"This is western Queens, from Newtown Creek up to Bowery Bay," Christie said. "That's the area we are interested in caring for. This area is clearly much too large for a small group to cover, so when we started the committee my thought was to complement and extend what the parks groups do by working on the approaches to the parks. We've done work on Broadway, because if people are coming to Socrates Park for maybe a movie night or to Hallets Cove to go kayaking, they will get off the subway at Broadway and 31st Street and walk down Broadway. We recently worked on trees along the perimeter of Rainey Park.

"Many of these trees are well established, and they don't need a lot of care, so we took one of the side streets and have been working on the trees there. We meet once a month—about six or seven of us, and we are out there for about two hours. We meet for coffee first and schmooze a little and then we get going. After we work, we need to find a place to dispose of the debris. Some members of the group come by bicycle, and they load branches on the bike with bungee cords and walk them to a park. You can leave branches and tree debris in a park by prior arrangement with the Parks Department, and they will pick it up. If they have a chipper, like Astoria Park, you can leave the stuff in a pile, and they'll use the chipper to make mulch. Socrates Park doesn't have a chipper, but they will take very small pieces for their compost heap. The Two Coves Community Garden has acquired a tricycle cart with a flatbed on the back. They delivered compost to us one day when we were working on a tree pit."

Christie's shopping cart filled with 36 liters of water for the trees in her Astoria neighborhood

I asked Christie about watering. "I haven't gone out with other people to water, but I encourage the members of my group to water," she said. "There are 12 volunteers in my group. Some are enthusiastic but maybe 6 are out there watering trees on a regular basis. I also look at my trees for signs of vandalism, and if someone has tried to break off a branch and left it hanging, I'll call 311 if it's too large for me to handle."

The Parks Department responds almost immediately to her 311 calls to report vandalism. Parks' workers show up and help the tree in need.

"I've had success stories too," Christie said. "There was a business on a corner on 30th Avenue, and the tree pits had been newly bricked in. I went to the shop and spoke to the woman who was renting the shop. I said I wanted to speak to the building owner and left my information. He called, and I identified myself as a volunteer. I said that the tree would not do well with the brick completely covering the soil. I suggested that if he took out some of the bricks it would be better for the tree so that the roots could get air and water. He said he bricked over the soil because he thought it would be good for the tree: it would keep foot traffic off and keep dogs away. At the time, he thought it was a good idea, and it probably cost him money to do that. A couple of weeks later he had completely removed the bricks. I was so happy."

Tree stewardship involves weeding, watering, and pruning. Christie had taken the citizen pruner and tree steward workshops at Trees New York and bought tree pruning and tree care tools with her own money. She showed me her tools. "When I go out to water I always take my cart, which has the Green Shores NYC sign, so that people know what I'm doing and it gives me some street cred. I take a kneeler [a pink, rubbery mat to protect her knees], in case I need to do some weeding and trash bags. I usually take my two standard tools: my folding saw and hand pruner, which I put in my belt so I don't step on them. I always take gloves, and in my bag I have duct tape, because sometimes there's a Treegator with a hole in it. You don't know until you put water in it, but if there's a hole, you slap some duct tape on it and the next time you come by you can put on a fresh piece to plug that hole. There's always a weeder, pliers, and wire cutters in my bag too.

"If a support wire has been left on the tree as it grows," she continued, "it will start to girdle the tree, and it's not that easy to get off. So you can grab and twist with the pliers, and you can cut with the wire cutter. You just have to worry it off. I found these tools useful. I also carry garden gloves and latex gloves."

Christie took out a pole lopper, which gives her a longer reach, and a pole saw, which also allows her to reach higher branches that need to be sawed off. She pointed out that "it's important that your tools are appropriate for your strength. There are tools that are heavier and extend farther, but I don't have the upper body strength, so there's no sense in my getting those."

Christie carries a small bottle of alcohol and a rag to clean her tools when she's out in the field to avoid spreading a pest or disease from tree to tree. She also cleans them as soon as she gets home and applies 3-in-One oil to keep them oiled and in good, cutting condition. The citizen pruner course through Trees New York taught her how to care for tools. She received a list of ancillary supplies from friends who volunteer at Gantry Park in Long Island City. She noted that people who work with trees tend to be good, kind, and generous. I heartily agreed and remarked on how friendly and outgoing people were in the different neighborhoods I explored as I searched for tree species and their addresses.

Christie also takes a hard hat and goggles with her to protect her head and keep sawdust out of her eyes when she is sawing a high branch. A bright orange vest is part of her outfit, so that drivers will see her if she is pruning near the street. Christie showed me a mattock and a "claw" for loosening soil.

Christie led Trudy and me on a walk around her neighborhood. The first tree we came to was a Callery pear, which she says is in its third season. "This is one of the trees I started stewarding after I heard about 'Million Trees.' There were four new trees on the block; this one and its sister trees."

We approached a tree needing care, Christie said that she would clean it up later by removing dead branches. She thinks about how the tree will look in five years, "If the branches are growing too close together, you think about which is the healthier branch: which is the dominant one, which is the one that will do better, and then you remove the weaker. You start off looking for dead, damaged, and diseased branches. Then you look for 'crossing'—branches that have crossed over each other—and you leave the dominant branch, removing the other branch so the dominant branch has more room."

We arrived at a sycamore maple tree with a robin's nest. The tree had many bare branches, and Christie acknowledged that the tree was struggling. We noticed some healthy honey locusts from which Christie and her group had pruned an enormous amount of dead branches.

I asked Christie whether any young people were involved with Green Shores NYC, and she said volunteers ranged from their thirties through seventies.

When Christie was describing how she got involved with trees, she remembered the day she showed up to take the citizen pruner class, and Sam Bishop, director of Education for Trees New York, told the class, "You are going to become crazy about trees. Your friends are going to hate to see you coming, because that's all you're going to talk about." Christie turned around, looking at the other students, and thought, "Who is he talking to?" "Now," Christie said, "I know who he's talking to. And I don't know why I feel this way. I have no background in science or ecology."

Christie Van Kehrberg is a great friend to the trees of her neighborhood in Astoria, Queens. She is the queen of tree care tools and head of the street tree committee of Green Shores NYC. We learned so much from the short time we spent with her: about tree care, tree care tools, and individual generosity.

At the end of our tour, Christie showed us an unusual tree, which she referred to as her "raggedy-ass tree." She had been looking after it even though she didn't know what kind of tree it was. Something about it spoke to her. It looked like a "Dr. Seuss" tree, something you would see alone on an island with bare branches sticking out in every direction. We couldn't identify it. The bark was bright green with lenticels, leaves were compound, and it had flat bean pods. Christie said that this was a tree she watered every week and really wanted to see survive. Later in the week I sent photos of this tree to Wayne Cahilly at the New York Botanical Garden who identified it as an *Amur maackia*, a tree native to Manchuria. Christie was thrilled to finally have her tree identified.

Staten Island

Trudy and I met John Kilcullen in front of a century-old American elm on Monroe Avenue in the Tompkinsville section of Staten Island. This elm is considered to be one of the Great Trees of New York City. Great Trees are trees of unusually large size, shape or history. John frequently gives "Great Tree" walks in Staten Island where he both lives and works as an urban forester for the New York City Department of Parks and Recreation. John helps to monitor and care for Staten Island's street trees. He chose Tompkinsville and nearby St. George for us to explore because of their proximity to the Staten Island Ferry terminal. It is a five-minute walk from the ferry to these leafy neighborhoods. He told us about treating American elms as a preventive measure against Dutch elm disease.

"This American elm is one of two here in the neighborhood that we treated for Dutch elm disease," he said. "The Parks Department does that for American elms to protect them from *Ophiostoma*, a fungal disease that causes the tree to shut down. There was a contract to treat all the trees. It's an antifungal treatment that's injected into the root flare, where the trunk meets the soil. A needle-like instrument is drilled in and a plastic injector cap is pushed in and the fluid is flushed through the tree's vascular system. You do it every six inches around the tree until the tree takes all the fluid up. This is preventive to help the tree resist fungus. When we find American elms that appear to be healthy, we don't know if the tree has a natural resistance or if the tree has escaped a visit from the elm leaf beetle. The elm leaf beetle transmits the disease when it chews. The saliva goes into the tree and that's how it's transmitted. This American elm could have escaped the disease if there were no other diseased elms in proximity or no elm leaf beetles around. Many people think that most American elms are affected by this disease, but there are many that are resistant."

John estimates that this American elm is at least one hundred years old. He mentioned that houses in the Tompkinsville neighborhood where this tree has grown up, were built around the turn of the last century—late 1890s to early 1900s.

ROOT RAIN—A WATERING SYSTEM

As we walked along Monroe Avenue, we noticed a small, open circular pipe with a perforated cover going into the ground next to each newly planted tree. I asked whether these were part of a watering system. John said it was called *Root Rain*, a tree irrigation system the Parks Department's Forestry Division was testing. Surface roots can cause sidewalks to buckle. Root Rain can help roots spread out below the surface. Perforated pipes are placed at the base of the root ball of the tree. Water is directed down into soil so that the tree will establish roots deep into the soil. The small holes in the pipe aboveground allow water and air to get in but stop debris from falling through.

Newly planted trees are guaranteed to live for two years by the contractor—the nursery the city buys the trees from—and the contractor agrees to water each tree for the first two years of its life. With so many thousands of newly planted trees, contractors can't always keep up with the watering needs of

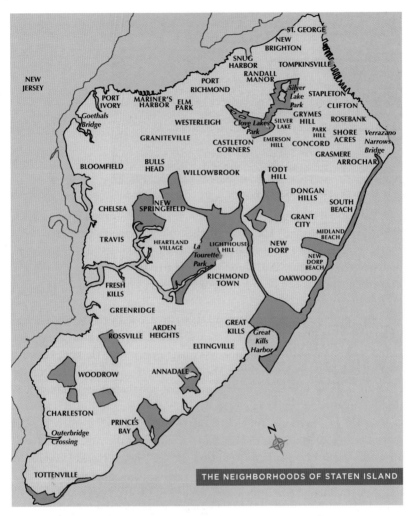

THE NEIGHBORHOODS OF STATEN ISLAND

these trees, particularly in the hot, dry summer of 2010. Residents are encouraged to pour water down the Root Rain pipes, at least 20 gallons a week, when it doesn't rain.

John wants to encourage tree stewardship and hopes that interested tree stewards visit the MillionTrees NYC website (www.milliontreesnyc.org) and the New York City Department of Parks & Recreation website (www.nycgov parks.org). "Tree stewardship in the first five years of a tree's life is critical," he said. In the past, many street trees didn't make it to maturity, but John hopes that, "with these initiatives to get the new trees established, in a few years, you're going to have major green blocks throughout the city."

Part of the Root Rain irrigation system

We noticed the large tree pits on Monroe Avenue surrounding the newly planted trees. John said, "The larger tree beds allow for more rainwater absorption and better root growth, and secondarily allows the planting of noncompeting flowering plants and, therefore, more tree stewardship in the process. Previously, tree pits had been five feet by five feet, which doesn't really allow much planting space."

We came upon a newly planted katsura tree, one of the 50 species featured in this book, and I noted that the tree looked like it was struggling. John, however, pointed out that the tree was doing pretty well. He said, "Look at next year's buds, they are all there. There's a little stress from the drought: the dried-up leaf edges. But it's pushing new leaves, and the winter leaf buds look healthy, so overall it's performing pretty well."

As we walked along, there were a few littleleaf linden trees. I asked John how he differentiated the littleleaf lindens from the American lindens. He pointed out that the branches of the litleleaf linden stayed close to the trunk as they ascended, whereas the American linden branches spread out gracefully from the trunk. John said that the littleleaf is more widely planted. No one had ever explained these differences so clearly to me.

We approached an enormous *Ginkgo biloba* tree on Fort Hill Circle. John said, "This tree is really great because it shows the diversity of the ginkgos. Lots

Large ginkgo with a double trunk and wide canopy, St. George, Staten Island

White mulberry tree spans Van Duzer Street in Staten Island

of ginkgos will have a center lead (trunk). This has a very broad canopy because it has two trunks."

I asked John whether he thought they cut the tree earlier in its life because of the electrical wires that went right between its two trunks. "I think it was a twin lead to begin with," he said, "and I don't see any evidence of a cut. It just worked out that there were twin leads and the wires were subsequently added."

We came upon a row of enormous silver maple trees, and John told me about the Parks Department's Trees and Sidewalks Program, where the city repairs sidewalks pushed up by tree roots for the homeowner and preserves the tree. "It's a very popular program, but it is difficult to get to every location. We worked on this sidewalk. In this older neighborhood, you have a lot of problems with tree roots pushing up sidewalks. The silver maple is no longer planted, because it grows so fast and tends to lift up the sidewalk."

We got back into our cars, and John guided us up and down the hills of St. George and led us to another one of its Great Trees: a white, male mulberry whose canopy spanned the cobblestone street. John explained, "This mulberry is dioecious; meaning there's a male and a female tree. This is a male and there-fore has no berries." Mulberries are sweet and delicious, enjoyed by humans, birds, and other wildlife, but once the berries fall on cars and the sidewalk, they turn everything purple. The tree was huge, dwarfing the quaint homes it shaded.

John intimately knows the street trees of Staten Island. He kindly showed us where we could find the different species featured in this book, and when-ever he could, he led us to a Great Tree.

2

TREE
TERMINOLOGY

Trees

TREE A perennial plant with a woody stem (the trunk) that attains the height of at least 15 or 20 feet.

> **Small tree:** 30 feet or under
>
> **Medium tree:** 85 feet or under
>
> **Large tree:** More than 85 feet

CONIFER A cone-bearing tree, usually evergreen with needle leaves. Some deciduous conifers are, notably, the bald cypress and dawn redwood trees, which lose their needle leaves each autumn.

EVERGREEN Trees with needle leaves that remain green and on the tree throughout winter.

DECIDUOUS Trees that lose their leaves each autumn.

Leaves

LEAF The tree's organ that manufactures food through a process known as *photosynthesis*. Leaves vary in shape from species to species, which is why people tend to identify trees by their leaf shape. However, some species have similar leaves and require close examination to see the differences.

CHLOROPHYLL Pigment inside cells of leaves that gives leaves their green color and where photosynthesis takes place.

PHOTOSYNTHESIS The process plants use to make food. Leaves take in sunlight, water, and carbon dioxide in the presence of chlorophyll and produce sugar, which is food for the tree, and oxygen as a by-product, which is the gas that all animals breathe.

BROADLEAF Flat, flexible, and thin leaves.

NEEDLE LEAVES Can live on the tree from two to five years before falling off, giving trees with needle leaves the name "evergreen." Needle leaves can be long or short, flat or roundish, narrow or overlapping. Needle leaves often have a waxy surface that holds in water year round and that protects leaves in winter from cold, and in summer from disease and pests.

LEAF STALK Attaches the leaf to the twig. It leaves a scar when it falls off.

LEAF SCAR The mark left on the twig when the leaf's stalk falls off in autumn.

LEAF TEETH The serrated edge of a leaf margin.

ENTIRE MARGIN When the leaf's edge has no teeth.

LEAF VENATION The shape and pattern of the leaf's veins.

PINNATE VEINS Feather shaped.

PALMATE VEINS   Palm shaped.

COMPOUND   Leaves made up of many leaflets attached to a single leaf stalk.

PINNATE COMPOUND   Feather-shaped compound leaves.

PALMATE COMPOUND   Palm-shaped compound leaves.

SIMPLE   Leaves made up of a single leaf blade.

LOBED   Simple leaf with indentations.

UNLOBED   Simple leaf with no indentations.

LEAF ARRANGEMENT   How the leaves are arranged on the twig or branch.

OPPOSITE   Leaves are arranged directly across from one another.

ALTERNATE   Leaves are arranged in an alternating pattern.

LEAF BRACTS   Modified leaves often found at the base of the tree's flowers.

Flowers

TREE FLOWERS   The reproductive organs of the tree.

MONOECIOUS   Trees having both male and female flowers.

DIOECIOUS   Male and female flowers are on separate trees.

STAMINATE   Pollen-producing male flowers.

PISTILLATE   Fruit-producing female flowers.

PISTIL   Contains female organs—stigma, style, ovary, and eggs.

STIGMA   Sticky top of the flower that attracts pollen.

STYLE   Holds up the stigma.

OVARY   Contains unfertilized eggs. Once eggs are fertilized, the ovary becomes the fruit and the eggs become the seeds, holding the new plant's embryo within.

EGGS   Contain the female DNA of the plant.

STAMEN   Contains male organs—filament, anther, and pollen.

FILAMENT   Slender, threadlike structure that supports the anther.

ANTHER   Small caps sitting atop the filament, which produce and hold pollen.

POLLEN   Contains sperm, which hold the male DNA of the plant.

PETALS   Often colorful, fragrant, showy part of flower that attracts pollinating insects, and other animals.

SEPALS   Enclose the flower bud, protecting it. When flower opens, sepals often sit below the petals.

PEDICEL   Flower stalk.

POLLINATORS   Animals attracted to a flower's color, scent, and shape collect its nectar and pollen. They then carry pollen to the next flower, which fertilizes that flower's eggs, allowing the plant to reproduce.

POLLINATION   When the pollen grain grows a pollen tube from the stigma through the style into the ovary to the eggs.

FERTILIZATION   Sperm within the pollen move through the pollen tube and enter the eggs, bringing the male flower's DNA to the egg.

Fruit and Seeds

GERMINATION   When the plant emerges from the seed and starts to grow.

GYMNOSPERMS   Seed-bearing plants whose seeds form on the outside of cones, not on the inside of fruit.

CONE   Female reproductive organ of gymnosperms, containing seeds on the outside of scales. Both bald cypress and dawn redwood trees produce cones.

ANGIOSPERMS   Seed-bearing plants whose seeds are enclosed within a fruit.

FRUIT   The part of the plant that contains the seeds. The ripened ovary becomes the fruit. Deciduous trees bear several types of tree fruit.

SEEDPODS   Usually long and narrow fruit of legumes, containing seeds. Honey locust, black locust, and eastern redbuds have seedpods.

SAMARAS/KEYS   Winged fruit. Maple trees and ash trees produce samaras.

SEED BALLS   Round, often spiky balls containing seeds. Sweetgum trees and London plane trees produce seed balls.

DRUPE   Fleshy fruit with hard layer surrounding the seed. Crabapples and Callery pears produce drupes.

NUTS   Extremely tough seed cover. Oak trees and horse chestnuts produce nuts.

Bark, Twigs, and Branches

BARK   Protective woody layer covering the trunk, branches, and twigs.

TWIGS   Slender branch or shoot of tree.

BRANCHLET   Small branch.

EXFOLIATING BARK   Peeling bark. London plane trees have bark that peels off during the growing season as the trunk and branches grow horizontally.

LEAF SCARS The patterned mark left on a twig after a leaf and its stem falls off. The base of the stem attached to the twig creates this mark.

LATERAL BUDS Winter leaf buds that grow from the sides of the twig.

TERMINAL BUDS Winter leaf buds that grow from the end of the twig.

LENTICELS Horizontal breathing pores on the bark and twigs of trees.

3

ILLUSTRATED
GLOSSARY

LEAF ARRANGEMENTS

DECIDUOUS LEAVES

alternate

opposite

LEAF TYPES

compound

simple

compound
pinnate

compound
palmate

ANATOMY

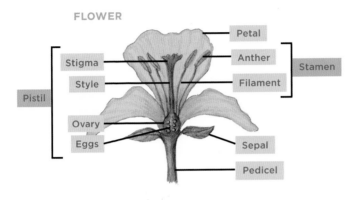

Petal

Stigma

Anther

Style

Filament

Stamen

Pistil

Ovary

Eggs

Sepal

Pedicel

TWIG

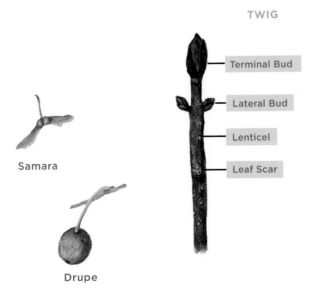

Terminal Bud

Lateral Bud

Lenticel

Leaf Scar

Samara

Drupe

4

TREES

BALD CYPRESS: *Taxodium distichum*

WHERE TO SEE

Bronx: Across from 1001 East 164th Street, Morris Park
Brooklyn: 546 East 17th Street, Midwood
Manhattan: 323 East 65th Street, Upper East Side
Queens: Northern Boulevard between Union Street and Parsons Boulevard, Flushing High School, Flushing
Staten Island: Corner of Richmond Terrace and Snug Harbor Road, Snug Harbor

WHAT'S IN A NAME? This deciduous conifer loses its needle leaves in autumn, making it look "bald."

HEIGHT Large, attaining a height of 130 feet with a pyramidal shape.

CROWN SHAPE Pointy when young but broadly round on mature trees. The trunk has a buttressed, wide, flaring base, which tapers into a narrower form. Branches can be widespread and drooping, providing cover for waterfowl and other birds.

BARK 1- to 2-inch-thick, reddish-brown ridges, fibrous and surprisingly soft to the touch.

TWIGS Deciduous, alternate, slender, pliable, pale yellow green, and shiny when young, turning light reddish brown as tree matures.

WINTER LEAF BUDS Tiny, round, covered with overlapping light brown scales.

LEAVES Deciduous, feather-like needles are small, pale yellow green, slightly curved and pointed, "2-ranked," or across from one another on either side of the twigs.

FLOWERS Male and female flowers are on the same tree. Male catkins hang in slender, drooping purple clusters, 3–5 inches long that can be seen during winter. Tiny female cones develop singly or in clusters of two or three. They are fertilized by pollen released by male cones in March and April.

FRUIT Round fertilized female cones, attached by a very short stem to the twig, are green at first but mature into brownish purple by mid- to late autumn. Each cone consists of 9–16 four-sided scales, which fall off after maturity. Each scale carries two triangular seeds.

PLATE I Bald Cypress

HABITAT Bald cypresses love water and wet soil, but they do well on city streets.

ECOLOGICAL VALUE When growing near water, the tree produces bulbous, woody "knees" sticking up out of the water or wet soil. These extend from the roots and are thought to help the tree take in oxygen when the roots are submerged in swampy water. Squirrels, songbirds, wild turkeys, egrets, herons, and ducks consume seeds. As squirrels feast on the cones, uneaten scales fall to the soil where the seeds within can germinate into new trees. Often called "eternal wood," the bald cypress wood does not easily rot, which is why it is used to build water tanks atop apartment houses in New York City.

Bald cypress branch, needle leaves, and cones

Bald cypress trees line
Northern Boulevard behind
Flushing High School

| DECIDUOUS CONIFERS

Bald cypress cone

Bark of the bald cypress can feel surprisingly soft to the touch

DAWN REDWOOD: *Metasequoia glyptostroboides*

WHERE TO SEE

Bronx: 9 Shore Road, in front of Bronx Riding Stables, Pelham Bay

Brooklyn: 151 Willow Street, Brooklyn Heights

Manhattan: 140 West 85th Street, Upper West Side

Queens: Corner 15 Greenway Terrace South, Forest Hills Gardens

Staten Island: Richmond Avenue at the Staten Island Mall, New Springville

WHAT'S IN A NAME? Derived from Greek, *glypto* (to carve) and *strobus* (cone) referring to the patterned cones.

HEIGHT Fast-growing, enormously tall, growing up to 150 feet.

CROWN SHAPE Pyramidal with a straight, tall trunk when young; as it ages, the crown rounds out. The trunk can develop a buttressed base as it matures.

BARK Reddish brown, stringy, fibrous, exfoliating in strips with a stringy or ropelike appearance.

TWIGS Opposite, slender, light reddish brown, smooth compared with the trunk's bark. Some twigs are deciduous: shaped like pinnately compound leaves; nondeciduous twigs: short, tan, opposite, cylindrical, and sticking out at right angles. Deciduous stems fall to the ground with the needle leaves in autumn.

WINTER LEAF BUDS No buds on deciduous stems; nondeciduous or persistent stems hold opposite buds.

LEAVES Deciduous, opposite, linear, needle-like, 1-inch long, flat, and two-ranked on either side of the twig. Feathery, yellowish green, turning reddish brown in autumn.

FLOWERS Males and female flowers separate on the same tree: females are yellowish green, standing singly and erect, covered in fused scales; males, pale yellowish brown, in slender hanging clusters up to a foot long.

FRUIT Long stemmed, green, turning brown in autumn, four-sided, squarelike cones with small, winged seeds, suspended on 1-inch-long, round stalks.

HABITAT Tolerant of all kinds of city soils.

ECOLOGICAL VALUE Metasequoias, which once covered much of the Northern Hemisphere, were thought to have been extinct for millions of years until they were discovered in the 1940s, growing in China. They can grow several feet per year and reach more than 150 feet. Now they are planted as street trees and will be planted in several sites in the city to memorialize emergency workers who perished on 9/11.

PLATE 2   Dawn Redwood

Dawn redwoods stand tall in front of the Bronx Riding Stable on Shore Road

Cone of the dawn redwood hangs from a long stalk

Reddish-brown fibrous bark of the dawn redwood

Newly planted dawn redwood tree behind Louis Brandeis High School on West 85th Street, Manhattan

CALLERY PEAR: *Pyrus calleryana*

WHERE TO SEE
Bronx: 211 Ditmars Street, City Island
Brooklyn: 150 Montague Street, Brooklyn Heights
Manhattan: 254 West 73rd Street, Upper West Side
Queens: 159-16 Laburnum Avenue, Flushing
Staten Island: 43 Monroe Avenue, Tompkinsville

WHAT'S IN A NAME? Joseph Callery, a French missionary, "discovered" this tree in China in 1858.

HEIGHT A small to medium tree, which can grow to 60 feet.

CROWN SHAPE Round with a straight trunk and ascending branches narrowly angled close to the trunk.

BARK When young, smooth, light brown, and covered with lenticels (breathing pores); with age, grayish brown with narrow, scaly ridges.

TWIGS Shiny brown to reddish brown.

WINTER LEAF BUDS Large terminal buds covered with light-brown hairs.

LEAVES Simple, alternate, heart shaped with finely serrated margins, 2–3 inches long, shiny green above, pale below, turning a gorgeous scarlet, orange, yellow, purple, and bronze in autumn; sometimes fall leaves can have all of these colors at once.

FLOWERS Dense, showy white flower clusters emerge before leaves in April or in early May, covering New York City streets in an explosion of white blossoms.

FRUIT Small, round, hard, greenish brown with pale dots, softening after winter.

HABITAT Thrives in urban conditions.

ECOLOGICAL VALUE A beautiful tree in every season, it is one of the most common street trees in New York City. Fruit is consumed by birds and squirrels. A Callery pear that was nearly destroyed at the World Trade Center on 9/11 was rescued and nurtured by the New York City Department of Parks and Recreation. Now known as the "Survivor Tree" and replanted at Ground Zero, President Obama placed a wreath near this tree in May 2011.

PLATE 3 Callery Pear

Callery pear starting to bud

Snowy white blossoms of
Callery pear trees on West
78th Street, Manhattan

Leaves and olive-brown fruit of the Callery pear

Callery pear tree's fall foliage

NORTHERN CATALPA: *Catalpa speciosa*

WHERE TO SEE

Bronx: Grand Concourse between 164th and 165th Streets, Concourse
Brooklyn: 573 Marlborough Road, Midwood
Manhattan: 529 West 217th Street, Inwood
Queens: 5900 block of 164th Street, Flushing
Staten Island: 219 Curtis Place, St. George

WHAT'S IN A NAME? Native Americans referred to this tree as the *catawba*.

HEIGHT Grows rapidly up to 70 feet.

CROWN SHAPE Spreading branches, irregular and rounded crown.

BARK Depending on the individual tree, the mature catalpa bark can have ridges, plates, or scales.

TWIGS Raised white lenticels (breathing pores) and round, sunken leaf scars dot the twig; leaf scars are in a whorled arrangement of three, making this tree easy to identify in winter.

WINTER LEAF BUDS Small, scaly buds, with no terminal leaf buds present.

LEAVES Large, simple, alternate, heart-shaped leaves are 6–12 inches long and 4–5 inches wide. They emerge in whirls of three around the twig (thus the three leaf scars in a whorled arrangement on the twig), and hang suspended from long petioles (leaf stems). Leaves have entire margins (no serrated edges). They are dark green above, paler and hairy below.

FLOWERS Flower clusters contain gorgeous, showy, simple flowers with frilled, fused white petals dotted with purple and yellow spots and lines.

FRUIT 12 to 24 inches long, thin, pendulous, green seedpods turn brown in fall, giving this tree the name *cigar tree*. Within these long structures are hundreds of small, fringed seeds, which spill out as the pod splits open lengthwise when it falls to the ground in spring.

HABITAT Does well in dry, wet, or poor soil. Native to Mississippi, this tree can withstand intense summer heat.

ECOLOGICAL VALUE This beautiful tree is interesting in every season. In late spring, it produces lovely, showy flowers, which produce long, thin, hanging fruit that persists throughout winter into early spring. Cultivated by farmers in the Midwest, the catalpa is used for fence posts because the wood resists rot.

PLATE 4 Northern Catalpa

Northern catalpa tree, near Sunnyside Gardens, Queens

Yellow- and purple-spotted
catalpa flowers

Catalpa seedpods can grow 2 feet long

Scaly catalpa bark

SCHUBERT CHOKECHERRY: *Prunus virginiana*

WHERE TO SEE

Bronx: 495 City Island Avenue, City Island
Brooklyn: 123 Pierrepont Street, Brooklyn Heights
Manhattan: 1 West 131st Street, Harlem
Queens: Corner Roman Avenue and Greenway Terrace, Forest Hills Gardens
Staten Island: Side of 78 Fort Place, St. George

WHAT'S IN A NAME? Chokecherry refers to the bitter taste of the unripe fruit.

HEIGHT A small, fast-growing tree, chokecherry grows to 26 feet.

CROWN SHAPE Crooked trunk and irregular crown.

BARK Smooth, deep reddish brown or grayish brown, with shallow fissures as it matures.

TWIGS Slender reddish or orange brown, quite shiny, becoming darker as the tree matures.

WINTER LEAF BUDS Tiny (½ inch long) rounded tip, broad base, and covered with reddish-brown scales.

LEAVES Simple, alternate, serrated, with fine, sharp teeth along the margins; ovate, up to 2 inches wide and 4 inches long, with short pointed tip and a tapered round base; shiny dark green above, paler below. In the Schubert cultivar, illustrated here, the green leaves turn deep purple red in summer.

FLOWERS 3- to 6-inch-long clusters of small flowers, each with five white, rounded petals.

FRUIT Red, black, or yellow, round, ⅖ inch, shiny, and fleshy.

HABITAT Tolerates a wide variety of soils.

ECOLOGICAL VALUE An important native tree for wildlife, the ripened fruit in autumn attracts more than 25 species of songbirds. If you are in a borough with white-tailed deer, they will browse the young twigs and new leaves. The tart fruit is used to make jellies and preserves.

PLATE 5   Schubert Chokecherry

Schubert chokecherry tree starting to bloom, City Island Avenue, the Bronx

Chokecherry flowers appear in clusters up to 6 inches long

In summer, the Schubert chokecherry's leaves turn dark red; seen here along with its fruit

Midsummer chokecherry tree, Pierrepont Street, Brooklyn Heights

KWANZAN CHERRY: *Prunus serrulata*

WHERE TO SEE
Bronx: 532 City Island Avenue, City Island
Brooklyn: 509 East 16th Street, Midwood
Manhattan: 303 West 78th Street, Upper West Side
Queens: 29-19 Broadway, Astoria
Staten Island: 13 Targee Street, Stapleton

WHAT'S IN A NAME? Kwanzan is an anglicized name for an Asian mountain near the native range of this tree.

HEIGHT This small- to medium-sized tree grows 25–35 feet tall and wide.

CROWN SHAPE Rounded, and spreading, making the tree appear wider than it is tall.

BARK Thin, shiny, reddish brown to bronze, smooth, with large, horizontal lenticels (breathing pores).

TWIGS Thick, reddish brown, covered in lenticels.

WINTER BUDS Large, reddish buds covered by several scales.

LEAVES Alternate, up to 5 inches long, serrated, broad in the middle, coming to a long, sharp point. Leaves emerge while flowers are still in bloom. Turning the most beautiful shades of crimson, orange, wine, and purple in autumn.

FLOWERS Showy, deep pink, double blossoms, 3–5 flowers in a cluster along the twig.

FRUIT This tree is sterile and typically produces no fruit.

HABITAT Tolerates most urban soil conditions.

ECOLOGICAL VALUE This tree is beautiful year round. Gorgeous, huge, deep-pink blossoms in spring. Large green leaves in summer give way to autumn hues, which rival the rainbow of colors of sugar maple leaves in fall. In winter, the red twigs and winter buds stand out in the ice and snow.

PLATE 6 Kwanzan Cherry

Kwanzan cherry tree in bloom, West 78th Street, Manhattan

Clusters of deep pink
Kwanzan cherry tree flowers

Autumn leaves of the Kwanzan cherry tree are among the most beautiful of the fall foliage

Kwanzan bark is covered in horizontal lenticels, which help the tree breathe

CRABAPPLE: *Malus* (VARIOUS SPECIES)

WHERE TO SEE

Bronx: Corner of 154th Street and Grand Concourse

Brooklyn: 496 East 17th Street, Midwood

Manhattan: 2222 Broadway at West 79th Street, Upper West Side

Queens: 1 Station Square, Forest Hills Gardens

Staten Island: Forest Avenue and Silver Lake Road, Randall Manor

Note: With hundreds of crabapple cultivars, we focus on common characteristics.

WHAT'S IN A NAME? In Old English, *crabbed* meant cranky or nasty: the tiny apples have a sour taste.

HEIGHT This small-sized tree grows 20–40 feet.

CROWN SHAPE Thick, open, round, gnarled "fairy tale" trunks and branches.

BARK Flaky, fissured, gray brown.

TWIGS Grayish brown, with circular bud scars. Some species have thorns.

WINTER BUDS Small, pointed.

LEAVES Alternate, simple, 2–4 inches, spoon shaped with long midvein from leaf stem to tip, with serrated margins. Leaves can be somewhat lobed along the margins.

FLOWERS Bearing five petals, flowers hang suspended from side shoots in small clusters. Dark pink buds appear in April, and flowers unfold in shades of white and pale or deep pink as leaves emerge when temperatures rise in mid-April to early May. Buds seem to last for weeks, and then, one warm spring day, they all pop open at once. Their lovely fragrance is carried for blocks.

FRUIT Varies in size from ¼ to ¾ inch in diameter and range from yellowish green to red. Shape also varies from oval to round.

HABITAT Drought tolerant and well suited to urban soil.

ECOLOGICAL VALUE Sour, bitter fruit makes sweet jellies and cider. Widely planted for their beautiful flower displays in spring, more than 20 species of songbirds, game birds, squirrels, and small mammals devour the tiny apples throughout fall and winter. It is believed that flocks of robins and other formerly migrating birds stick around in winter because there are so many crabapples to feed on. Throughout the year, small birds hide in the dense

PLATE 7 Crabapple

Crabapple tree covered in blossoms, Broadway Mall median,
West 79th Street, Manhattan

American robin perches on a crabapple bough
covered in pink and white blossoms

Crabapple flowers

Red and orange crabapples, a food source for New York City birds in autumn

DOWNY SERVICEBERRY: *Amelanchier arborea*

WHERE TO SEE
Bronx: 1105 Tinton Avenue, Morrisania
Brooklyn: 400 block of State Street, Boerum Hill
Manhattan: Riverside Boulevard at West 68th Street at top of ramp to
Riverside Park South, Upper West Side
Staten Island: 37 Monroe Avenue, Tompkinsville

WHAT'S IN A NAME? *Amelanchier* is Latin for "blood red," referring to the
color of the immature twigs. Named serviceberries because they ripened
when traveling preachers held outdoor revival meetings in rural areas of
nineteenth-century America.

HEIGHT A small tree, serviceberry grows up to 40 feet.

CROWN SHAPE Can have a narrow, round, or irregular crown.

BARK Light gray and smooth when immature, developing narrow ridges
and furrows as it matures.

TWIGS Reddish brown and slender.

WINTER LEAF BUDS ⅕ inch long, pointed, covered in reddish-brown to
yellowish-brown scales.

LEAVES Simple, alternate, serrated, fine-toothed margins, narrowly ovate,
up to 2 inches wide and 4 inches long, densely hairy, darker green above,
paler green below, turning yellow to red in autumn.

FLOWERS Showy, starlike, with five slender, white petals emerging in
terminal clusters before the leaves come out in early spring.

FRUIT Up to ½ inch green to red to reddish purple as they mature. Fleshy
and looks like a small apple, this fruit is edible but is absolutely adored by
birds and other wildlife: berries disappear quickly. I have seen song sparrows
devouring the fruit.

HABITAT Tolerates a wide variety of soil. Prefers moist, well-drained soil.

ECOLOGICAL VALUE Another common name for this tree is *shadblow*.
It flowers when the American shad migrate up the Hudson River from the
Atlantic Ocean to spawn in spring. *Juneberry* is yet another common name,
referring to the berries that ripen in summer. This is a valuable native tree.
The beautiful flowers attract pollinators, the berries provide nutritious food
for hungry birds, and the foliage is beautiful in every season, particularly
autumn.

PLATE 8   Downy Serviceberry

Downy serviceberry tree, West 68th Street and Riverside Boulevard

Flowers of the downy serviceberry appear in June when the shad migrate back into the Hudson River, giving the tree another common name: shadblow

Reddish-purple serviceberries fill the trees in autumn

A song sparrow rests after a meal of serviceberries

EASTERN REDBUD: *Cercis canadensis*

WHERE TO SEE

Bronx: Across from 911 Walton Avenue, Concourse Village
Brooklyn: 1304 Ditmas Avenue, Midwood
Manhattan: 315 East 7th Street, Lower East Side
Queens: 42 Summer Street, Forest Hills Gardens
Staten Island: Side of 42 Royal Oak, on Lakeland Road, Castleton Corners

WHAT'S IN A NAME? This tree's name reflects its northern range, *canadensis,* Canada.

HEIGHT A small tree growing to 30 feet.

CROWN Its small trunk, or trunks, and spreading branches form a low, broad crown.

BARK Thick, with narrow, scaly ridges.

TWIGS Slender, brown, smooth, slightly angled, or zigzagged.

WINTER LEAF BUDS Round, tiny, covered in reddish-brown scales.

LEAVES Large, dark blue green, alternate, heart shaped, 3–5 inches long and wide, with smooth, untoothed margins. They are suspended straight out from the zigzagged branches, giving the tree a delicate, yet densely full appearance.

FLOWERS Gorgeous lavender pink, pea-like "red bud" flowers appear on branches and trunk before the leaves in April.

FRUIT 2 to 4 inches long, flat, hanging seedpods, green at first, turning brown in the fall.

HABITAT Rich, moist soil.

ECOLOGICAL VALUE This small, native, understory tree is a legume and has nitrogen-fixing bacteria living in nodes in its roots. Many birds consume its seedpods, including northern cardinals, ring-necked pheasants, rose-breasted grosbeaks, and bobwhites. White-tailed deer and gray squirrels also feed on the seeds. Early spring flowers are a source of nectar for bees. Birds, such as the American robin, build their nests in the redbud's low branches.

PLATE 9   Eastern Redbud

Newly emerged, heart-shaped eastern redbud leaves

Delicate pink redbud flowers
grow from the branch

In autumn, eastern redbud seedpods turn brown

Reddish-brown bark of the eastern redbud

AMERICAN ELM: *Ulmus americana*

WHERE TO SEE
Bronx: 422 City Island Avenue, City Island
Brooklyn: 72nd Street and Ridge Boulevard, Fort Hamilton
Manhattan: 421 West 154th Street, Washington Heights
Queens: Side of 175 Ascan Avenue, Forest Hills Gardens
Staten Island: 121 Monroe Avenue, Tompkinsville

WHAT'S IN A NAME? *Ulmus* is Latin for elm.

HEIGHT Tall, attaining a height of 100 feet.

CROWN SHAPE Graceful, spreading, vase shaped, sometimes weeping.

BARK Thick, with deep furrows intersecting broad, flat ridges, creating diamond shapes or a woven, crisscross look to the bark.

TWIGS Slender, graceful; reddish brown when young, gray when mature.

WINTER LEAF BUDS Small, with broad bases and sharp tips, covered in tiny reddish-brown, slightly hairy scales.

LEAVES Alternate, 3–6 inches long, 1–3 inches wide, with uneven bases, widest near or above the middle, tapering to a point, with double coarse teeth on the margin. Leaves are dark green, smooth to rough above and pale and smooth to hairy below.

FLOWERS Small, suspended on long, drooping stems in three to five clusters per stalk. American elms do not flower until they are at least 35–40 years old.

FRUIT Flat, oval keys, broad across the middle, ⅕ to ½ inch long, deeply notched tips, hanging from long stalks. Keys are smooth, have hairy edges, and develop in great abundance from winter leaf buds before leaves emerge.

HABITAT Does well in most soil types.

ECOLOGICAL VALUE An important native tree whose seeds are loved by birds, squirrels, mice, deer, and rabbits. Seeds fall in great abundance in late spring/early summer and are eagerly consumed by city birds. Once widely planted on city streets, Dutch elm disease has destroyed many elms. The disease is caused by a fungus carried by bark beetles that arrived from Europe in trees imported to manufacture a type of veneer. Although many trees have been cut down, wonderful stretches of elms still stand, including long lines along Fifth Avenue, bordering Central Park, and Riverside Drive, bordering Riverside Park in Manhattan.

PLATE 10   American Elm

This massive American elm on the corner of Central Park
West and 77th Street had room to spread out. Its roots
have pushed up the cobblestone sidewalk

| DECIDUOUS BROADLEAF: SIMPLE, UNLOBED

Tiny, delicate American elm flowers

American elm keys fringed in white "hairs" with deeply notched tips

Thick, deeply furrowed American elm bark

CHINESE ELM: *Ulmus parvifolia*
(also known as the LACEBARK ELM)

WHERE TO SEE
Bronx: 422 Minnieford Avenue, City Island
Brooklyn: Corner of Clinton Avenue and 3rd Place, Carroll Gardens
Manhattan: 134 west 82nd Street, Upper West Side
Queens: 139-19 109th Street, Woodhaven
Staten Island: 125 St. Marks Place, St. George

WHAT'S IN A NAME? The alternative name *lacebark* refers to the beautiful patchwork-colored bark.

HEIGHT This medium-growing elm can attain a height of 50 feet, with a crown spreading just as wide or wider.

CROWN SHAPE Round and spreading, making this an excellent shade tree.

BARK Exfoliating (shedding) bark exposes exquisite brown, green, gray, and orange patches outlined by tiny orange lenticels. The beauty of this bark increases with maturity.

TWIGS Slender, smooth, reddish brown to gray, slightly zigzagged.

WINTER LEAF BUDS Small, reddish brown.

LEAVES 1 ½–2 inches long, dark green, shiny with rounded, serrated margins, unequal bases, and a deep midvein. Autumnal colors of red and purple appear in late November.

FLOWERS Wind-pollinated, small, yellow-green clusters, late summer / early fall within the leaf axils.

FRUIT ½-inch-long, brown, flat, oval keys with notched tips are produced in autumn and litter the ground in abundance in fall, unlike most other elms, which fruit in spring.

HABITAT Native to China, Japan, and Korea, this tree thrives in urban environments; well adapted to most soil types.

ECOLOGICAL VALUE Resistant to Dutch elm disease and air pollution. Planted for the beauty of its bark, spreading crown, and autumnal leaf colors.

PLATE II   Chinese Elm

Chinese elm tree on 3rd Place, Carroll Gardens, Brooklyn

Leaves and keys of the Chinese elm

Orange patches exposed beneath peeling
Chinese elm bark

Chinese elm bark is dotted with orange lenticels

JAPANESE ZELKOVA: *Zelkova serrata*

WHERE TO SEE
Bronx: 172 Ditmars Street, City Island
Brooklyn: 123 Pierrepont Street, Brooklyn Heights
Manhattan: 75 Riverside Drive, Upper West Side
Queens: 143-44 Quince Avenue, Flushing
Staten Island: 4 Knox Place, Castleton Corners

WHAT'S IN A NAME? Zelkova is derived from languages of the Caucasus: *dzel* (beam) and *kva* (rock). Zelkova was used for making long-lasting house beams.

HEIGHT Rapid grower when young and then moderate growth up to 80 feet.

CROWN SHAPE This tree has a pronounced vase shape, with branches ascending from the straight trunk and reaching out to form a round, spreading crown up to 60 feet wide.

BARK Smooth, shiny, reddish brown when young, with large lenticels (breathing pores), maturing to a showy bark that is mottled gray, pink, and orange.

TWIGS Slender, reddish brown to grayish brown, zigzagged.

WINTER LEAF BUDS Winter buds are at wide angles from the stems.

LEAVES Serrated, slightly rounded, sawtoothed margins, narrowly ovate, up to 1 inch wide and 3 inches long, dark green turning beautiful colors in fall, from orange to burgundy.

FLOWERS Tiny, inconspicuous, green. Male flowers are found at the base of new, lower leaves; female flowers are found near the upper leaves.

FRUIT Tiny, green, round, kidney-bean-shaped drupes hidden by the leaves, form in late spring, and mature by October.

HABITAT Zelkova is a great urban street tree as it tolerates compacted soil, poor drainage, air pollution, and drought.

ECOLOGICAL VALUE This large tree is a fast grower and will provide decades of shade and beauty on city streets. Many zelkovas were planted to replace diseased elms as they are a member of the elm family, yet do not succumb to Dutch elm disease.

PLATE 12 Japanese Zelkova

Autumn foliage of the zelkova tree, Riverside Drive, Upper West Side

Zelkova leaves and flowers

Among the leaves can be seen the small green fruit of the zelkova

Note the horizontal lenticels on the zelkova bark

FLOWERING DOGWOOD: *Cornus florida*

WHERE TO SEE
Bronx: 5824 Fieldston Road, Fieldston
Brooklyn: 1120 Ditmas Avenue, Midwood
Manhattan: Riverside Drive at West 77th Street, just inside Riverside Park
Queens: 157-38 Quince Avenue, Flushing
Staten Island: 1000 Richmond Terrace, Snug Harbor/Randall Manor

WHAT'S IN A NAME? *Cornus* is Latin for "hard wood," a feature of this tree.

HEIGHT A beautiful small tree growing 30-45 feet.

CROWN SHAPE Spreading upright branches create either a pyramidal or rounded crown.

BARK Small, angular scales and fissures, grayish brown.

TWIGS Smooth, slender, pale green to reddish green becoming reddish brown and covered by leaf scars with age.

WINTER LEAF BUDS Leaf and flower buds develop in summer.
Leaf buds are covered with two scales and are thin and cone shaped;
flower buds are rounder and covered with four scales.

LEAVES Simple, opposite, broader near the base or in the middle, up to 6 inches long and 2 inches wide, with a pointy tip. Leaf veins follow the curve of the margins, which are often entire or wavy. Leaves are thick, dark green above and pale below, turning a brilliant red in autumn.

FLOWERS The interesting and surprising flowers are actually tiny florets with four yellow-green petals, packed densely (15–20) in the center and surrounded by four large white to pale pink petal-like bracts, which most people mistake for the flowers.

FRUIT The tiny flowers produce clusters of brilliant red, oblong berries, which are an important and nutritious food for wildlife.

HABITAT Though sensitive to urban conditions, our flowering dogwoods seem to do well in the five boroughs, perhaps with some extra care from people on the block.

ECOLOGICAL VALUE The brilliant red fruit and red leaves act like beacons in autumn to attract migrating birds that feed on the highly nutritious berries. Squirrels, raccoons, and small mammals also feed on the fruit.

PLATE 13 Flowering Dogwood

Covered in blossoms, this little dogwood stands
on the edge of Riverside Drive and 77th Street

The flowering dogwood leaves have smooth
margins that can be wavy, but without teeth

Pink "petals" of the dogwood flower are really bracts that surround the true flowers: tiny yellow-green florets in the center

Next spring's flower buds appear alongside the dogwood's autumn leaves, which turn deep red early in the fall

GINKGO BILOBA: *Ginkgo biloba*

WHERE TO SEE
Bronx: 140 Bowne Street, City Island
Brooklyn: 71 3rd Place, Carroll Gardens
Manhattan: 268 West 73rd Street, Upper West Side
Queens: 138-46 Northern Boulevard, Flushing
Staten Island: 45 Fort Hill Circle, St. George

WHAT'S IN A NAME? The leaf of this tree may have two lobes, thus the species name *biloba* for bilobed.

HEIGHT Tall, attaining a height of 80 feet.

CROWN SHAPE Pyramidal and angular.

BARK Light brown to grayish brown, more deeply furrowed and ridged on mature trees.

TWIGS Smooth and tan, with spurs.

WINTER LEAF BUDS Small, with broad bases and sharp tips, covered in tiny reddish-brown, slightly hairy scales.

LEAVES Although a deciduous tree, it is related to conifers; its leaves have parallel veins, which some scientists believe evolved from the fused needles of evergreen trees. The fan-shaped leaves, attached to spurs on twigs, can be notched in the middle giving them a bilobed shape.

FLOWERS Ginkgos are dioecious with male and female flowers on separate trees. Male trees have hanging catkins, which pollinate female flowers suspended from 2-inch spurs, by means of "free-swimming" sperm, just like the ginkgo's more primitive, distant relatives, ferns, and mosses.

FRUIT Not a true fruit but a thickening of the seed coat, made up of sugars that nourish the developing embryo within the seed. Produced in great abundance on female trees, they are malodorous, flesh colored, and hang suspended from spurs. The ginkgo is a gymnosperm, producing "naked" seeds, not a fruit-producing angiosperm. There is no ovary; therefore, there is no fruit.

HABITAT Highly tolerant of urban conditions.

PLATE 14 Ginkgo Biloba

ECOLOGICAL VALUE Ginkgos are very long-lived, pest- and disease-free trees. One ancient tree in Hiroshima survived the atom bomb in 1945. Ginkgos are living fossils that have survived for 150 million years. Thought to have become extinct during the ice age, ginkgos were discovered in 1691 growing near temples in Japan. They are the single remaining species of a large group of plants that were once dominant around the world. The nut of the ginkgo tree is valued as a delicacy, sold as the "white nut" in Asian markets. Crows and eastern gray squirrels feed on ginkgo nuts.

Ginkgo leaf and flowers

Ginkgo "fruit" turn
orange in autumn

Golden ginkgo leaves ablaze in the morning sun on the Upper West Side

Deeply furrowed bark
of the ginkgo biloba tree

HAWTHORN: *Crataegus spp.*

WHERE TO SEE
Bronx: 211 East 205th Street, Norwood
Brooklyn: 400 block of State Street, Boerum Hill
Manhattan: St. Mark's Place and Avenue A, Lower East Side
Queens: Across from 37 Greenway Terrace, Forest Hills Gardens
Staten Island: Norway Avenue at McClean Avenue, Ocean Breeze/
South Beach

Note: With more than a thousand species of hawthorns and their ability to hybridize, we focus on common characteristics of this ancient and historic little tree.

WHAT'S IN A NAME? *Haw* is a word for berry, referring to its small, apple-like fruit. The twigs bear thorns, hence, hawthorn.

HEIGHT Small tree, grows up to 25 feet.

CROWN SHAPE Dense, shrublike, with rounded crown.

BARK Grayish brown and smooth when young; covered in small scales with age.

TWIGS Zigzagged, bearing thorns.

WINTER LEAF BUDS Round, dark brown.

LEAVES Simple, alternate, serrated, with shallow to deep lobes.

FLOWERS This tree is often covered in clusters of white, pink, or red, five-petaled flowers in April or early May.

FRUIT Small, yellow, green, or red, produced in profusion, and loved by birds.

HABITAT Tolerates most types of soil and does well in urban conditions.

ECOLOGICAL VALUE Dense, thicket-like branches offer cover and nesting sites for birds and small mammals. Fruit are consumed by birds. Hundreds of insect species feed on the nectar and fruit, and many live within the bark. In Celtic folklore, the hawthorn is known as the "fairy bush." It is believed that fairy spirits guard the tree and that it is bad luck to cut one down.

PLATE 15   Hawthorn

Hawthorn tree, Avenue B, edge of Tompkins Square Park

White, five-petaled flowers
of the hawthorn tree

Red berries of the hawthorn, ripening in autumn, are consumed by birds

Hawthorn bark is a patchwork of grays and browns

EUROPEAN HORNBEAM: *Carpinus betulus*

WHERE TO SEE
Bronx: 993 Tinton Avenue, Morrisania
Brooklyn: 52 Third Avenue, Boerum Hill
Manhattan: 117 West 72nd Street, Upper West Side
Queens: Across from 20 71st Avenue, Forest Hills
Staten Island: Henderson Avenue between Clinton and Tysen Streets,
Snug Harbor / New Brighton

WHAT'S IN A NAME? Another common name for this tree is *ironwood*,
referring to the very strong wood that can blunt metal tools used to cut
into it.

HEIGHT Slow growing, can reach 60 feet with a 40-foot spread.

CROWN SHAPE Oval or vase shaped with delicate branches that can reach the
ground and multiple trunks.

BARK Smooth, sinewy, muscle-like, and dark gray.

TWIGS Thin, brown, delicate, and covered in lenticels (breathing pores).

WINTER LEAF BUDS Long, tapered, reddish brown, partially curved
around twigs.

LEAVES Alternate, deciduous, highly textured, almost pleated, 2 ½ to 5
inches long and 1–2 inches wide, oblong with round base, sharp tip, and
double-toothed margins. Dense, dark-green leaves turn yellow in fall.

FLOWERS 1 ½-inch-long, pendulous, green male catkins, tinged with red,
and flared female catkins emerge with new leaves at the end of twigs in April.
Male and female flowers are on the same tree.

FRUIT Female catkins form multiple chainlike clusters of hanging, three-
lobed, yellow-green leaf bracts, which bear small nutlets.

HABITAT Tolerates many types of soil and urban conditions.

ECOLOGICAL VALUE A long-lived tree with an interesting muscular look to
its bark. Squirrels and birds feed on the nutlets in autumn. The wood is dense
and hard and was used as yokes for oxen in Europe.

PLATE 16   European Hornbeam

Hornbeam catkins hang in profusion in early spring

Hornbeam clusters of three-lobed bracts bearing tiny nutlets

Hornbeam bracts with nutlet

Fluted, muscular bark
of the hornbeam

JAPANESE TREE LILAC: *Syringa reticulata*

Bronx: 640 Minnieford Avenue, City Island
Brooklyn: 477 East 16th Street, Midwood
Manhattan: 137 Avenue B, Lower East Side
Queens: 10-48 46th Road, Astoria
Staten Island: 78 Fort Place, St. George

WHAT'S IN A NAME? Most lilacs are shrubs, unlike this "tree lilac."

HEIGHT Small tree, attaining a height of 20–30 feet.

CROWN SHAPE Dense, oval, sometimes with multiple trunks.

BARK Grayish brown, shiny with horizontal lenticels (breathing pores), cherry tree-like.

TWIGS Thick, opposite, forking, shiny brown, streaked with lenticels.

WINTER LEAF BUDS Opposite, large, oval, orange brown.

LEAVES Opposite, large, 5 inches with rounded leaf bases and entire margins, sometimes heart shaped; no teeth but wavy leaf edges as leaves curve down in a folded V shape. Dark green leaves emerge in early spring.

FLOWERS Large, up to a foot-long terminal clusters of creamy white, fragrant flowers.

FRUIT Green to yellow tan, ¾-inch, upright capsules in large panicles.

HABITAT Tolerates poor urban soil.

ECOLOGICAL VALUE This tree is beautiful throughout the seasons. In early spring, large opposite leaves emerge, followed by huge, white flowers in summer, which produce large pale-green capsules that turn golden brown and persist throughout winter.

PLATE 17 Japanese Tree Lilac

Enormous clusters of creamy white flowers of the
Japanese tree lilac emerge in midsummer

Green fruit of the Japanese tree lilac
appear in large panicles in autumn

Pale, horizontal lenticels dot the
Japanese tree lilac's bark

KATSURA: *Cercidiphyllum japonicum*

WHERE TO SEE
Bronx: 975 Walton Avenue, Concourse
Brooklyn: Across from 941 Washington Avenue, Prospect Lefferts Gardens
Manhattan: 170 West 78th Street, Upper West Side
Staten Island: Side of 61 Victory Boulevard on Monroe Avenue,
Tompkinsville

WHAT'S IN A NAME? This tree was named for the Katsura district of
Kyoto, Japan.

HEIGHT Medium, fast growing, can reach 60 feet.

CROWN SHAPE Multi-trunked, creating a pyramidal, round-shaped,
dense crown.

BARK Unique, ornamental, peeling, narrow tan and brown strips.

TWIGS Slender, reddish brown, with tan lenticels (breathing pores).

WINTER LEAF BUDS Tiny, reddish brown, angled toward twig.

LEAVES Opposite, 3-inch, very round, heart-shaped, scalloped margins,
purple to bronze in early spring; blue green in summer; red to gold in autumn
when they exude a sweet fragrance.

FLOWERS Pale green to red male and female flowers on separate trees.
Male flowers are smaller than female, which are wind-pollinated.

FRUIT ¾-inch-long pods appearing in clusters of two to four along twigs;
release seeds in October.

HABITAT Tolerates many types of soil except for drought and compaction.
Native to wet regions; this tree needs a lot of water.

ECOLOGICAL VALUE Dense leaves provide good cover for birds and their
nests. This tree is beautiful in every season. New spring leaves are reddish
purple or bronze; summer leaves are blue green; autumn leaves turn scarlet
to brilliant yellow, and in winter its interesting bark stands out. Katsura tree
seeds were brought to America in 1865 when Thomas Hogg Jr., a diplomat
to Japan appointed by President Lincoln, sent home seeds to his family-run
nursery in Manhattan.

PLATE 18 **Katsura**

Ornamental vertical gray and tan strips mark the bark of the Katsura tree

Red flowers appear on the Katsura tree in early spring

Clusters of Katsura pods mature in autumn

Round, heart-shaped Katsura leaves appear opposite each other on the twig

AMERICAN LINDEN: *Tilia americana*

WHERE TO SEE
Bronx: 173 Bowne Street, City Island
Brooklyn: 62 3rd Place, Carroll Gardens
Manhattan: 276 Riverside Drive, Upper West Side
Queens: 31-22 29th Street, Astoria
Staten Island: 210 Victory Boulevard, Tompkinsville

WHAT'S IN A NAME? *Tilia* is Latin for linden.

HEIGHT A fast-growing, fairly long-lived tree attaining a height of 100 feet, with a straight trunk and branches generally appearing halfway up the trunk.

CROWN SHAPE Large and spreading. Branches arch upward or outward, giving the tree a stately look.

BARK Smooth and light brown on young trees; darker, deeply furrowed, and crisscrossed on mature trees.

TWIGS Yellowish brown, slender with zigzag shape.

WINTER LEAF BUDS Reddish, in two rows along the twig, 2 inches long with overlapping scales. There are no terminal buds.

LEAVES Simple, alternate, 6–7 inches long and 3–4 inches wide, with broad, uneven, heart-shaped bases; the leaves taper to a point with coarse, sawtoothed margins. Leaves are dark green above and pale below. In cool early spring or late autumn days, the margins curl underneath.

FLOWERS Cream colored, opening in late June with a heady fragrance that can be detected for blocks. Walking up the subway steps into a fragrant early summer evening in New York City is made memorable when these wonderful flowers are in full bloom. Several small flowers hang suspended from a slender stem, which is also attached to a 4- to 5-inch-long bract (modified leaf).

FRUIT Flowers produce small, round nutlets. When mature the bract attached to the flower stalk spins as it floats through the air, carrying the seeds to the ground, where they might germinate, producing new American linden trees.

HABITAT Tolerates most urban soil types.

PLATE 19   American Linden

ECOLOGICAL VALUE A beautiful shade tree, American linden seeds are eaten by squirrels, mice, and game birds such as bobwhites. Native Americans used the tough inner bark to fashion a tangle-free rope and finer threads; Iroquois carved masks from the soft, light-colored sapwood. Yama, a Japanese sculptor who lived at the 79th Street Boat Basin for many years, created massive sculptures from fallen linden trees he found in Riverside Park. He appreciated the soft, beautiful, easy-to-carve wood.

Spring leaves of the American linden about to emerge from their buds

Creamy yellow American linden flowers are attached to bracts

American linden nutlets attached to their bracts

Soaring trunk of the
American linden

LITTLELEAF LINDEN: *Tilia cordata*

WHERE TO SEE
Bronx: 440 City Island Avenue, City Island
Brooklyn: 1422 Ditmas Avenue, Midwood
Manhattan: 417 Grand Street, Lower East Side
Queens: 157-17 Rose Avenue, Flushing
Staten Island: Across from 97 Monroe Avenue, Tompkinsville

WHAT'S IN A NAME? Species name *cordata,* refers to the heart, in this case to heart-shaped leaves.

HEIGHT A slow grower, this tree can attain a height of 80 feet.

CROWN Dense, pyramidal to round, supported by one trunk or several. Young trees' branches are angled close to the trunk. Mature trees' lower branches bend toward the ground, giving it a graceful shape

BARK Young tree is grayish brown with shallow furrows. At maturity, bark becomes dark gray with deep furrows and large ridges.

TWIGS Smooth, reddish brown, zigzagged, and dense.

WINTER LEAF BUDS Large, shiny, reddish brown.

LEAVES 2 ½ inches long and wide, simple, alternate, dark green above, paler below with a wide, heart-shaped base. Leaves are arranged in a dense manner along the branches, providing deep shade.

FLOWERS Just like the American linden, the cream-colored clusters of flowers create a heavenly smell in late June and early July, which can be detected blocks away. They are suspended from a slender bract (modified leaf).

FRUIT Flowers produce small, round nutlets that hang from the bracts, which spin to the ground in autumn when nutlets mature.

HABITAT Tolerates urban conditions and all types of soil but prefers moist soil.

ECOLOGICAL VALUE Native to Europe and western Asia, this beautiful tree provides dense shade in summer, fragrant flowers in late spring, and a graceful form all winter. The leaves turn a lovely yellow in autumn.

PLATE 20 Littleleaf Linden

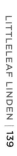

Littleleaf linden branches ascend close to the trunk

Pale yellow flowers are extremely fragrant in late spring, early summer

Littleleaf linden leaves and nutlets in early autumn

Fissured trunk of litleleaf linden tree

SILVER LINDEN: *Tilia tomentosa*

WHERE TO SEE
Bronx: 241 City Island Avenue, City Island
Brooklyn: 148 Montague Street, Brooklyn Heights
Manhattan: 245 West 72nd Street, Upper West Side
Queens: 79 Groton Street, Forest Hills Gardens
Staten Island: 45 Belmont Place, St. George

WHAT'S IN A NAME? This tree is called a silver linden because the underside of the leaf is silvery.

HEIGHT A fast grower with a height up to 70 feet.

CROWN SHAPE Pyramidal and rounded at the top.

BARK Light gray, smooth when young, ridged and furrowed with maturity.

TWIGS Somewhat thick, zigzagged, greenish or reddish, slightly hairy.

WINTER LEAF BUDS Rounded, scaly, with fine hairs, angled to side of twig.

LEAVES Simple, alternate, serrated, dark green above, silver and quite hairy below, 2–5 inches long, yellow in autumn.

FLOWERS Incredibly fragrant clusters of 7–10 creamy white flowers bloom in late June through early July. Each flower cluster attached to leafy bract by long stem.

FRUIT Small, 3/8-inch-oval, egg-shaped nutlets, attached to leafy bract. When fruit is mature, this bract breaks free and twirls like a helicopter blade as it carries nutlets to the soil to germinate.

HABITAT Tolerates poor urban soil conditions, including moderate drought but favors moist soil.

ECOLOGICAL VALUE This beautiful tree is perfect for city streets as it tolerates pollution and full sun. Its flowers provide nectar and pollen for bees and other pollinating insects, and the flowers' heady fragrance and beautiful leaves, glinting silver in the wind, delight city dwellers every summer.

PLATE 21   Silver Linden

Silver linden leaves, dark green above, silvery below

"Hairy" underside of
silver linden leaf

Silver linden flowers and bracts against the silvery underside of the leaves

When nutlets mature, the bracts drop from the tree like little helicopters, carrying the seeds to the ground

SAUCER MAGNOLIA: *Magnolia × soulangiana*

WHERE TO SEE
Bronx: 605 Minnieford Avenue, City Island
Brooklyn: 480 East 17th Street, Midwood
Manhattan: 2382 Broadway, Upper West Side
Queens: Corner of Greenway Terrace and Slocum Crescent,
Forest Hills Gardens
Staten Island: 150 Daniel Low Terrace, St. George

WHAT'S IN A NAME? Magnolia was named in honor of eighteenth-century French botanist Pierre Magnol.

HEIGHT A small but beautiful tree growing to 25 feet.

CROWN SHAPE Spreading branches create a wide-spreading crown.

BARK Smooth and pale gray.

TWIGS Pale gray and thick.

WINTER LEAF BUDS Enormous, "furry" buds, covered in dense hair slowly opening in April. Right before they open they are almost as showy and beautiful as the fully opened flowers.

LEAVES Simple, alternate, up to 8 inches long and 4 inches wide, broadest toward the short, pointy tip; green above and hairy below.

FLOWERS Enormous, showy, up to 10 inches long with six large, pink, purple, or white petals, opening up like wide saucers singly, and at the end of twigs; can be fragrant.

FRUIT Conelike, up to 4 inches long, rosy pink, and made up of multiple scarlet red, two-seeded fruits, which have short points at the tip, curving outward; maturing in autumn.

HABITAT Thrives in well-cared-for city medians, like Manhattan's Broadway Mall in the West 70s and 80s.

ECOLOGICAL VALUE This magnolia is a hybrid between two Chinese species: yulan magnolia (*Magnolia heptapeta*) and lily magnolia (*Magnolia quinquepeta*), created in 1820.

PLATE 22 Saucer Magnolia

Saucer magnolia flower bud unfurling from its furry sepal

Huge flowers of the saucer magnolia tree

Conelike magnolia fruit emerge in late summer

Large red seeds erupt from the fruit and fall to the ground in early autumn

PURPLE LEAF PLUM: *Prunus cerasifera*

Bronx: 419 Minnieford Avenue, City Island
Brooklyn: 470 East 17th Street, Midwood
Manhattan: 37 Washington Square West, Greenwich Village
Queens: 47-39 158th Street, Flushing
Staten Island: 107 Monroe Avenue, Tompkinsville

WHAT'S IN A NAME? Translated *cerasifera* means "bearing cherry-like fruit."

HEIGHT A small tree, the purple leaf plum can attain the height of 25 feet.

CROWN SHAPE Vase shaped, with dense, round, and symmetrical crown.

BARK Red, brown, and orange scales, with horizontal lenticels (breathing pores) and lengthwise fissures making the bark look as if it is covered in reddish-brown squares.

TWIGS Slender, reddish brown.

WINTER LEAF BUDS Small, pointy tip, covered with reddish brown scales.

LEAVES Alternate, simple, deciduous leaves, ovate, coppery when they first emerge to reddish purple in summer and fall, with serrated margins. When they grow in full sun, they have the richest color; in shade, they turn reddish green.

FLOWERS Fragrant white or pink, with red stamens, flowering in early spring and attracting many pollinators.

FRUIT Purple, 1- to 3-inch-round drupes that birds, squirrels, and other small mammals feed on in summer.

HABITAT A hardy city tree, tolerant of many soil types.

ECOLOGICAL VALUE Beautiful foliage during the growing season, from spring through autumn, this little tree also produces lovely flowers, which feed hungry bees and other city pollinators in spring, and drupes, which feed birds and small mammals in summer and fall.

PLATE 23　Purple Leaf Plum

Purple leaf plum tree on the edge of Washington Square Park

Lovely purple leaf plum flowers emerge in early spring with the leaves

Colorful bark of the purple leaf plum tree, covered in red, brown, and orange scales

LONDON PLANE: *Platanus* × *acerifolia*

This is the most common tree in New York City.

WHERE TO SEE

Bronx: 444 Minnieford Avenue, City Island
Brooklyn: 68 3rd Place, Carroll Gardens
Manhattan: 37 Washington Square West, Greenwich Village
Queens: 39-30 46th Street, Sunnyside Gardens
Staten Island: 80 Fort Hill Circle, St. George

WHAT'S IN A NAME? Translated from Greek, *platanus* means broad and refers to the broad leaves. *Acerifolia* refers to the maple-like leaves (maples belong to the genus *Acer*).

HEIGHT Can grow to be enormous at 120 feet or more.

CROWN SHAPE Branches are huge and spreading, giving the tree a round or pyramidal shape.

BARK Gray; exfoliates, revealing cream, yellow, and green patches during the growing season when the bark peels off in large plates as the trunk and limbs grow horizontally.

TWIGS A slight zigzag pattern, green at first turning grayish brown with maturity.

WINTER LEAF BUDS Conical, lateral, and terminal buds are reddish brown and with a caplike scale. Side buds are covered by the bases of the long leafstalks. In late April, buds become huge before they burst open with their leaves.

LEAVES Alternate, simple, 5–7 inches long and wide, with three to five palm-shaped lobes, sometimes with a few large teeth, sometimes with none; darker green above, paler below.

FLOWERS Inconspicuous, green ball-like clusters, separate male and female flowers, often two per stalk, hanging in stringed groups of one, two, or three, which is a characteristic for identifying London plane.

FRUIT Purple, brown, bristly balls, mature in autumn and fall off the tree usually by February. These balls hang on a long stalk and are made up of many narrow nutlets surrounded by hair tufts.

HABITAT Extremely tolerant of city conditions: poor soil, drought.

PLATE 24   London Plane Tree

ECOLOGICAL VALUE Both Frederick Law Olmsted, in the late nineteenth century, and Robert Moses and the New York City Parks Department, in the twentieth century, planted London plane trees extensively throughout New York City. It is our most common street tree. The London plane is a hybrid of the American sycamore and the Oriental plane. In the early seventeenth century, the gardener to Charles I, King of England, brought seeds of the American sycamore back from Virginia. It is believed that the trees from these seeds hybridized with the Oriental plane trees in his garden and produced the London plane. The leaf of the London plane is the symbol of the Department of New York City Parks and Recreation. The seedpods fall off in late winter and are consumed by birds.

Baby red-tailed hawk in his nest high in a London plane tree

Seed balls hang suspended from the London plane in late summer

The patchy, colorful bark of the London plane after a rain. Bark flakes off as the tree grows, revealing patches of yellow, green, and gray beneath

Seed balls are composed of many nutlets surrounded by hairy tufts

HEDGE MAPLE: *Acer campestre*

WHERE TO SEE
Bronx: 550 Minnieford Avenue, City Island
Brooklyn: 155 Montague Street, Brooklyn Heights
Manhattan: 123 West 13th Street, West Village
Queens: 100-11 70th Avenue, Forest Hills
Staten Island: Across from 199 St. Mark's Place, St. George

WHAT'S IN A NAME? Another common name for this tree is *field maple.*

HEIGHT This nonnative maple species grows up to 35 feet, sometimes with multiple trunks.

CROWN SHAPE Very round with branches low to the ground.

BARK Grayish brown with shallow ridges.

TWIGS Some young twigs can have corky ridges.

WINTER LEAF BUDS Small, scaly brown.

LEAVES Simple, opposite, 2–4 inches long, 2–4 inches wide, three to five lobes, star shaped, dark green with a "melted" look to the margins (edges). When crushed, the leaf veins and stems exude a milky sap. Fall foliage is yellow.

FLOWERS Appearing in early spring, the small yellow-green flowers are found in clusters. Flowers, like leaves and samaras, are opposite each other on the twig.

FRUIT Twin samaras up to 1 ¾ inches long, join together to form a straight 180-degree angle.

HABITAT This maple tolerates air pollution, compacted soils, drought, and other tough urban conditions.

ECOLOGICAL VALUE It is the only maple native to England. This maple is an excellent street tree as it tolerates poor and compacted soil and provides dense shade.

PLATE 25   Hedge Maple

Large hedge maple soars over homes in City Island

Rounded lobes of the hedge maple leaves and their opposite samaras, which join to form a nearly straight line

Scaly bark of hedge maple tree

JAPANESE MAPLE: *Acer palmatum*

WHERE TO SEE

Bronx: 600 Minnieford Avenue, corner of Kilroe Street, City Island
Brooklyn: 1408 Ditmas Avenue, Midwood
Manhattan: Corner of 525 West End Avenue at West 85th Street,
Upper West Side
Queens: 47-20 158th Street, Flushing
Staten Island: 29 Monroe Avenue, Tompkinsville

WHAT'S IN A NAME? The leaf resembles an outstretched hand, thus the species name *palmatum*.

HEIGHT Small tree, reaching a height of 15–25 feet.

CROWN SHAPE Irregular to rounded; extremely graceful, often with multiple ornamental, "muscular" trunks. Young trees have a round, domelike shape. As trees mature, they develop a graceful, irregular shape.

BARK Thin, gray and green patches.

TWIGS Green to red and shiny; quite ornamental.

WINTER LEAF BUDS Red and opposite. Bases of leaf buds are surrounded by hairy, paper-thin sheaths.

LEAVES Opposite, 2–5 inches long, green to red, with five to nine narrow, toothed leaflets, arranged in a palm or star shape. Autumn colors are exquisite: brilliant reds, copper, orange, and gold.

FLOWERS Small, reddish purple, emerge on warm spring days.

FRUIT Pinkish-red to green samaras, opposite one another, and angled down.

HABITAT Adaptable to most soil types but prefer moist, well-drained soil. These small trees do not do well in windy spots.

ECOLOGICAL VALUE These little trees bring such beauty to our city. Their delicate leaves are exquisite throughout the growing season but particularly beautiful in fall. These trees typify the art and grace of Asian gardens. They are native to China, Japan, and Korea.

PLATE 26 Japanese Maple

Japanese maple in Flushing, Queens

Tiny red flowers of the Japanese maple appear in May

Red samaras of the Japanese maple

In autumn, the Japanese maple leaves are brilliant in sunlight

NORWAY MAPLE: *Acer platanoides*

WHERE TO SEE
Bronx: 151 Bowne Street, City Island
Brooklyn: 39 4th Place, Carroll Gardens
Manhattan: 285 Convent Avenue, Hamilton Heights
Queens: 25-21 31st Street, Astoria
Staten Island: 110 East Raleigh, West New Brighton

WHAT'S IN A NAME? This imported species not only is native to Norway but also has a natural range that extends to Iran.

HEIGHT A medium-tall tree, Norway maples attain a height of usually not more than 60 feet.

CROWN SHAPE Oval.

BARK Smooth on young trees; dark gray, developing shallow furrows and flat plates as tree ages.

TWIGS Smooth, green, turning reddish brown or red with age.

WINTER LEAF BUDS Small, $\frac{1}{10}$ to $\frac{1}{5}$ inch long, rounded at tip, and covered with overlapping red scales.

LEAVES Wide, simple, opposite leaves are 3–6 inches long and 3–8 inches wide, generally with teeth bearing five lobes, each tooth ending in a long bristle.

FLOWERS Appearing in early spring before the leaves. Greenish-yellow flowers are found in small clusters; each flower has five tiny petals and five sepals. The flowers with five to eight stamens are the males. Flowers, like leaves, are opposite each other on the twig.

FRUIT A double samara, or two wings, hanging opposite each other on the twig at almost 180-degree angle. The disk-shaped seeds lie within the samaras, close together at the center where the two wings meet.

HABITAT Tolerate most soil types and city pollution.

ECOLOGICAL VALUE New York City Parks Department considers the Norway maple, which was widely planted by city and park planners, to be an invasive tree, and it is often cut down and ripped out to make room for native trees. Mature Norway maples are beautiful trees that thrive in urban conditions because they are so hardy.

PLATE 27   Norway Maple

Norway maple flowers emerge before the leaves in early spring

Cluster of bright green Norway maple flowers

| DECIDUOUS BROADLEAF: SIMPLE, LOBED

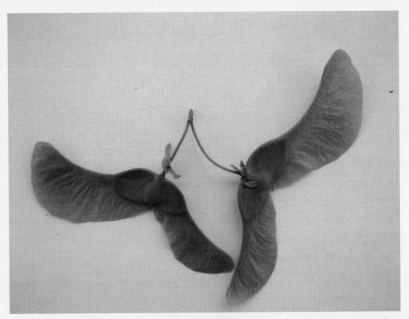

Norway maple samaras are angled away from each other

Bark of a mature Norway maple tree

RED MAPLE: *Acer rubrum*

WHERE TO SEE
Bronx: 430 City Island Avenue, City Island
Brooklyn: 228 Bay 40th Street, Bensonhurst
Manhattan: 518 West 135th Street, Hamilton Heights
Queens: 141-61 33rd Avenue, Flushing
Staten Island: 93 Monroe Avenue, Tompkinsville

WHAT'S IN A NAME? The species name *rubrum* is Latin for *red*. It is called a red maple for many reasons—the green leaves turn red in autumn; the tree has red leaf stems, flowers, and fruit; and in winter, the leaf buds are red.

HEIGHT A medium-tall tree, red maples attain a height of usually not more than 90 feet.

CROWN SHAPE Narrow to round.

BARK Smooth on young trees; dark gray, developing shallow furrows and flat plates as tree ages.

TWIGS Smooth, green, turning reddish brown or red with age.

WINTER LEAF BUDS Small, ⅒ to ⅕ inch long, rounded at tip, and covered with overlapping red scales.

LEAVES Simple, opposite, 2 inches long, 1 ½ to 4 inches wide, generally three lobes, occasionally five with two minor lobes at leaf base. Double toothed along the margin (leaf edge), with pointed tip and rounded base. Light green above, whitish green below, with red leaf stems.

FLOWERS Appearing in early spring before the leaves, the red flowers are found in small clusters with each flower having five tiny petals. The flowers with five to eight stamens are males. Flowers, like leaves, are opposite one another on the twig.

FRUIT A double samara, or two wings, hanging opposite each other on the twig: red, reddish brown, or greenish brown, ½ to 1 inch long and deeply angled toward the ground. The bulbous maple seed is within the samara, at the base of each wing, next to the red fruit stem.

HABITAT Red maples tolerate most soil types.

ECOLOGICAL VALUE Abundant seeds provide food for birds and squirrels and beauty for us. In winter, their red twigs and red leaf buds provide color. In early spring, red maple is one of the first trees to flower. The new summer leaves are red and the foliage is dense. In autumn, the leaves are aflame!

PLATE 28   Red Maple

Red maple flowers emerge before the leaves

Flowers produce red samaras that are opposite each other and angled down

Red maple trunk surrounded by its crown of autumn leaves

Few leaves are more colorful than the red maple in autumn

SILVER MAPLE: *Acer saccharinum*

WHERE TO SEE
Bronx: 426 Minnieford Avenue, City Island
Brooklyn: 619 Carlton Avenue, Prospect Heights
Manhattan: 122 Manhattan Avenue at West 105th Street
Queens: 160-17 Laburnum, Flushing
Staten Island: 2 and 11 Belmont Place, St. George

WHAT'S IN A NAME? The species name *saccharinum is* Latin for *sweet sap.*

HEIGHT Fast-growing, medium-tall tree attains a height of close to 100 feet.

CROWN SHAPE Spreading, round above a short, thick straight, trunk.

BARK Thin, smooth on young trees; grayish brown, developing shallow furrows and thin, flat plates as tree ages.

TWIGS Hanging, slender, green, turning reddish brown with age.

WINTER LEAF BUDS Overlapping reddish-brown scales; small ⅕ to ⅓ inch long, broadest near base or middle with round tips.

LEAVES Simple, opposite 5–8 inches long, 4–7 inches wide, deeply cut five lobes, narrow sinuses, and double-toothed margins. Leaves have pointed tips and square to heart-shaped bases. Color is bright green above and pale white to silvery below. The leaves are papery and hang from reddish, slender leaf stems.

FLOWERS Greenish-yellow male and female flowers on either same tree or different trees appear in late winter before leaves emerge. Flowers are opposite each other on the twigs, with three to seven stamens on the male flower and one hairy pistil on the female flower.

FRUIT Greenish-yellow double samara, or two wings, hang opposite each other on the twig: 1 ½ to 3 inches long and angled toward the ground: the largest fruit produced by any native maple.

HABITAT Thrives in moist, well-drained soil.

ECOLOGICAL VALUE Beautiful delicate foliage with silver undersides, this tree is short lived (140 years) and subject to loss of branches in stormy weather. Because of this, the silver maple offers winter dens for squirrels and raccoons. It produces copious amounts of seed eaten by squirrels, mice, and birds. Swelling winter leaf buds provide a source of nutritious food for hungry squirrels in late winter / early spring.

PLATE 29   Silver Maple

Mature silver maple tree's roots have grown over the curb in St. George, Staten Island

Note the deeply cut lobes of the silver maple leaves, shown here in autumn

Like all maples, silver maple leaves are opposite one another on the branch

Furrowed bark of the silver maple tree

SUGAR MAPLE: *Acer saccharum*

WHERE TO SEE
Bronx: 426 Minnieford Avenue, City Island
Brooklyn: 8858 20th Avenue, Bath Beach
Manhattan: McKenna Square, across from 510 West 165th Street, Washington Heights
Queens: 29-07 31st Avenue, Astoria
Staten Island: 1000 Richmond Terrace, Snug Harbor / Randall Manor

WHAT'S IN A NAME? A prized syrup tree, *saccharum* is Latin for *sweet*.

HEIGHT A large tree, with a thick, straight trunk, growing to 100 feet.

CROWN SHAPE The massive trunk and branches create a spreading round crown.

BARK Gray when young, developing fissures and ridges and turning dark gray with age with some pink showing through.

TWIGS Slender green when young, becoming orange to chestnut brown.

WINTER LEAF BUDS ½ inch long, cone shaped with a pointy tip and covered with chestnut-brown, mildly hairy, overlapping scales. The lateral buds are smaller than the terminal buds.

LEAVES Simple, opposite, 3–8 inches wide and long, with five palmate lobes bearing pointed tips. Several large teeth along the margins, with a broad, square base; thin, papery, bright green, and smooth above, paler below.

FLOWERS Yellowish green, with flowers having both male and female parts, hanging in long-stalked clusters of a few flowers just below the new spring leaves.

FRUIT The opposite and paired samaras (winged seeds) more than 1 ½ inches long and have a 60-degree angle between them.

HABITAT Thrives in most soil types if it has space for its roots to grow. Does poorly in small spaces with restricted soil area.

ECOLOGICAL VALUE The sugar maple can live for more than 250 years and provide delicious maple syrup if tapped. Birds, squirrels, and other small mammals love the seeds. The beautiful leaves of the sugar maple turn gorgeous shades of red, orange, and yellow in autumn.

PLATE 30 Sugar Maple

Gray fissured trunk of a mature sugar maple tree with pink inner bark

Brilliant leaves of the sugar maple in October

Sugar maple tree in City Island, the Bronx

SYCAMORE MAPLE: *Acer pseudoplatanus*

WHERE TO SEE

Bronx: Northwest corner of Ditmars Street and City Island Avenue, City Island

Brooklyn: Across from 1035 Washington Avenue, Prospect Lefferts Gardens

Manhattan: 58 West 130th Street, Harlem

Queens: 25-13 31st Avenue, Astoria

Staten Island: 518 Van Duzer Street, Stapleton

WHAT'S IN A NAME? *Pseudo* means *false*; thus, *pseudoplatanus* is the species name because its leaves resemble the leaves of a true sycamore (genus *Platanus*).

HEIGHT A large maple, sometimes growing up to 100 feet.

CROWN SHAPE Spreading branches form a round crown.

BARK Small, grayish-brown scaly plates with lovely orange underbark peeking out from beneath when plates fall off the showy trunk.

TWIGS Gray and smooth with lenticels (breathing pores).

WINTER LEAF BUDS Large, green, plump; terminal buds present.

LEAVES Large, simple, opposite, dark green, 3–7 inches wide and long with deeply recessed veins.

FLOWERS Greenish yellow, appearing in late spring; flowers are on 3- to 6-inch-long hanging clusters.

FRUIT Up to 2 inches long, the double, sometimes triple, samaras (winged seeds) hang in dense numbers, drooping at a 90-degree angle from one another.

HABITAT Sycamore maples tolerate most soil types and are highly salt tolerant, which is why they are planted and thrive in City Island on the Long Island Sound.

ECOLOGICAL VALUE This large tree is a fast grower and will provide decades of shade and beauty on city streets. Because of its ability to grow in full sun or partial shade and almost any soil type, this tree is considered an invasive species.

PLATE 31   Sycamore Maple

New spring leaves of the sycamore maple tree

| DECIDUOUS BROADLEAF: SIMPLE, LOBED

Samaras of the sycamore maple hang in long clusters in autumn

Sycamore maple samaras can sometimes come in triplets

Mottled gray and pink bark of the sycamore maple

WHITE MULBERRY: *Morus alba*

WHERE TO SEE

Bronx: 3639 Palmer Avenue, Edenwald
Brooklyn: 47A Willow Street, Brooklyn Heights
Manhattan: Convent Avenue and West 141st Street in front of St. Luke's Episcopal Church, Hamilton Heights
Queens: 25-09 Broadway, Astoria
Staten Island: 524 Van Duzer Street, Stapleton

WHAT'S IN A NAME? The berries of this tree turn from white to reddish purple.

HEIGHT A medium tree growing to 60 feet.

CROWN SHAPE Rounded, crown dense with twigs.

BARK Young bark is pale brownish orange with tiny lenticels (breathing holes); mature bark with ridges and scales and an orange inner bark exposed between the ridges.

TWIGS Red to orange, narrow.

WINTER LEAF BUDS Orange brown, rounded, angled toward twig.

LEAVES Large, 6 ½ inch, pale green, glossy, and smooth above, with rounded teeth along the margin. Leaves can be egg shaped, mitten shaped, or with several lobes.

FLOWERS Small, greenish female catkins emerge in early spring with the leaves; 2-inch-long male catkins are suspended from the twig. Some mulberry trees are dioecious; some are monoecious.

FRUIT Very sweet, white to reddish purple.

HABITAT Tolerant of poor urban soil.

ECOLOGICAL VALUE This is the mulberry tree that has been cultivated in China for several thousand years whose leaves are the host food for silkworms. It was brought over to America in early colonial times to start a silk industry. Although that failed, the trees spread throughout the east and south and provide sweet fruit for humans, birds, and other wildlife, and leaves for children, parents, and teachers raising silkworms.

PLATE 32   White Mulberry

Multiple trunks of the
white mulberry tree

Mulberry flowers emerge from
twigs bearing tiny white lenticels

Deeply cut lobes of the glossy white mulberry leaf

Fissured gray mulberry bark with orange inner bark peeking out

EASTERN WHITE OAK: *Quercus alba*

Bronx: Grand Concourse and East 64th Street, edge of Joyce Kilmer Park, Concourse Village
Brooklyn: 49 Willow Street, Brooklyn Heights
Manhattan: 25 and 27 Broadhurst Avenue, Hamilton Heights
Queens: Corner of Continental Avenue and Groton Street, Forest Hills Gardens
Staten Island: 4 Oak Court, Great Kills

WHAT'S IN A NAME? The species name *alba* means white, a reference to the whitish-gray bark often seen on mature trees.

HEIGHT Soaring at more than 100 feet tall.

CROWN SHAPE Rounded crown over a straight trunk.

BARK Thick, light gray with long fissures and narrow blocks and ridges.

TWIGS Hairy, reddish green when young; smooth and gray as tree ages.

WINTER LEAF BUDS Small and rounded, covered with smooth, reddish-brown scales.

LEAVES Grayish green to blue green, seven to nine rounded lobes, alternate, up to 8 ½ inches long with short leaf stalks.

FLOWERS Male and female flowers appear in early spring with the first leaves; 3-inch-long, yellow-green male catkins hang suspended from twigs, and inconspicuous, two to four reddish-brown female flowers lie within the axils of the leaf stalks. Flowers are wind pollinated.

FRUIT Oblong acorns up to 1 ¼ inches long bear shallow caps with bumpy scales. Green acorns turn brown with maturity. They are sweet and enjoyed by wildlife and germinate right after hitting the ground. Large acorn crops are produced every four to six years.

HABITAT Tolerates many types of soil but does best in well-drained soil.

ECOLOGICAL VALUE Eastern white oak acorns are an important food source for wildlife and are consumed by many animals, including white-tailed deer, squirrels, wild turkeys, and raccoons.

PLATE 33   Eastern White Oak

Eastern white oak giant in Riverdale, the Bronx

Rounded lobes of the white oak leaf with male catkin flowers

White oak acorns mature in one season, fall to the ground, and are consumed by wildlife

Fissured blocks of the eastern white oak's gray bark

ENGLISH OAK: *Quercus robur*

Bronx: Walton Avenue and East 167th Street, Concourse Village
Brooklyn: 501 East 17th Street, Midwood
Manhattan: 218 West 147th Street, Harlem
Queens: Across from 36-40 Bowne Street, Flushing
Staten Island: Richmond Terrace westbound between Hamilton Avenue and St. Peter's Place, St. George

WHAT'S IN A NAME? A good wood for timber, *robur* translated means strong.

HEIGHT A very large tree, growing more than 100 feet tall, the English oak also has a substantial trunk and massive, wide-spreading branches.

CROWN SHAPE Round and spreading, almost as wide as the tree is tall.

BARK Brownish gray and furrowed.

TWIGS Light brown when young; darker at maturity, terminating, like all oaks, in a cluster of leaf buds.

WINTER LEAF BUDS Large terminal buds; smaller lateral buds.

LEAVES 2 ½ to 5 inches long, with rounded lobes typical of trees in the white oak family. Leaves are wider toward the outer end and narrower toward the leaf stem. Leaves are 1 inch to 2 ½ inches wide, dark green throughout the summer, turning brown in autumn. Like many oaks, the tree holds on to its leaves throughout most of the winter.

FLOWERS Pale green male catkins hang from twigs in spring as new leaves appear along with tiny reddish-brown female flowers.

FRUIT Smooth oval-shaped acorns can be more than an inch long. The cup covers one-third of the nut. Acorns hang from long stems.

HABITAT Tolerates a range of soil types, drought, and moisture.

ECOLOGICAL VALUE This is the legendary oak of Europe, standing in Robin Hood's Sherwood Forest, worshiped by Celtic people and many others across the continent. Hulls and masts of sailing ships were made of the mighty English oak.

194 | DECIDUOUS BROADLEAF: SIMPLE, LOBED

PLATE 34   English Oak

Enormous English oak looms over
Bowne Street in Flushing, Queens

Luminous spring leaves of the English oak

Male catkins and rounded leaf lobes of the English oak

Long acorns with shallow caps mature in the first season

NORTHERN RED OAK: *Quercus rubra*

WHERE TO SEE
Bronx: 1204 Shakespeare Avenue, Highbridge
Brooklyn: 1308 Ditmas Avenue, Midwood
Manhattan: Across from 132 East 7th Street, Lower East Side
Queens: 36-19 Bowne Street, Flushing
Staten Island: 138 Royal Oak Road, Castleton Corners

WHAT'S IN A NAME? The wood is reddish and many of the leaf stems are red.

HEIGHT These fast-growing oaks can soar more than 90 feet with a trunk diameter of 2–4 feet.

CROWN SHAPE Round and spreading where there is room; narrower where space above the street is more limited.

BARK Young trees: smooth, greenish brown to reddish brown. Mature: dark brown with shallow fissures and broad gray ridges running vertically down the trunk.

TWIGS Smooth greenish brown to reddish brown.

WINTER LEAF BUDS ¼ inch long with pointed tips; the terminal buds are usually in a cluster of three or more.

LEAVES Simple, alternate, 5–8 inches long, 4–5 inches wide, with reddish leaf stems. Smooth, dark green above, pale green below with tufts of down in vein axils. Each leaf has 7–11 bristle-tipped lobes separated by shallow, V-shaped sinuses. Fall foliage: dark red to orange.

FLOWERS Yellowish-green hanging male catkins can be seen alongside tiny leaves as they emerge in spring. Small female flowers produce acorns.

FRUIT Shallow cup with large, reddish-brown, 1-inch-long acorn that requires two years to germinate.

HABITAT Tolerates pollution and poor soil.

ECOLOGICAL VALUE Excellent shade tree. Acorns are the primary source of food during the winter for squirrels, chipmunks, wild turkeys, white-tailed deer, blue jays, white-breasted and red-breasted nuthatches, chickadees, northern cardinals, and woodpeckers.

PLATE 35   Northern Red Oak

Huge crown of the northern red oak on West 79th Street below the West Side Highway

Delicate new northern red oak leaves
and male catkins emerge in spring

American robin in her nest beneath a canopy of northern red oak leaves

Northern red oak acorns are large with shallow cups

PIN OAK: *Quercus palustris*

WHERE TO SEE
Bronx: 437 Minnieford Avenue, City Island
Brooklyn: 147 Pierrepont Street, Brooklyn Heights
Manhattan: 425 West 144th Street, Hamilton Heights
Queens: 143-60 229th Street, Laurelton
Staten Island: 138 Royal Oak Road, Castleton Corners

WHAT'S IN A NAME? Pin oak wood was used as wooden pins, or pegs, in construction of wooden buildings.

HEIGHT Fast-growing trees, pin oaks can grow more than 80 feet, bearing a tall, straight trunk with a diameter of more than 3 feet.

CROWN SHAPE Lower branches droop, middle branches stand straight out horizontally, and top branches shoot up. This shape makes the pin oak easily identifiable.

BARK On young trees bark is thin, smooth, and grayish brown. On mature trees, bark has grayish-brown fissures, revealing reddish-brown inner bark.

TWIGS Thin, short with fine hairs; reddish brown when young; smooth and gray as they mature.

WINTER LEAF BUDS ¹⁄₁₀ inch long with tapered tips, covered by overlapping, reddish-brown scales.

LEAVES Simple, alternate, 3–6 inches long, 2–4 inches wide, and broad in the middle. Five to seven lobes with deeply cut C-shaped sinuses giving the leaves a narrow appearance. Papery, dark green, smooth, shiny above, pale beneath with hair tufts in the axils of main leaf veins.

FLOWERS Yellowish-green male catkins appear with emerging leaves in spring. Small female flowers produce acorns.

FRUIT Shallow cup encloses only the base of the small ½-inch-long acorn that requires two years to germinate. In autumn, these small acorns are covered in dark-green and light-green stripes.

HABITAT Tolerates wet or poorly aerated soil.

ECOLOGICAL VALUE A commonly planted city street tree. Acorns are the primary source of food during winter for squirrels, chipmunks, wild turkeys, white-tailed deer, ducks, blue jays, white-breasted and red-breasted nuthatches, chickadees, northern cardinals, and woodpeckers.

PLATE 36   Pin Oak

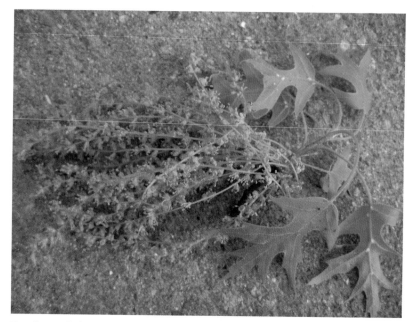

Deeply cut, C-shaped sinuses help identify the pin
oak leaves shown here with male catkins in late spring

Pin oak acorns are relatively small with very shallow cups

Gray fissured bark of the pin oak tree

Most oaks retain their leaves throughout winter. Notice the distinctive shape: lower branches, down; midbranches, straight out; top branches reaching upward

SAWTOOTH OAK: *Quercus acutissima*

WHERE TO SEE

Bronx: 675 Walton Avenue, Concourse Village
Brooklyn: 553 Westminster Road, Midwood
Manhattan: 176 West 105th Street, Upper West Side
Queens: 107-08 110th Street, South Richmond Hill
Staten Island: 2200 Richmond Avenue, Bulls Head

WHAT'S IN A NAME? This tree has saw-toothed leaf edges.

HEIGHT This East Asian, medium-sized oak can grow to more than 50 feet tall with a trunk diameter of 3 feet. Once established, it can grow 3 feet each year.

CROWN SHAPE Pyramidal when young, developing a rounded canopy as it matures, with a tall, straight trunk.

BARK Narrow gray ridges and furrows, even when tree is young. With age, bark becomes corky.

TWIGS Light brown when young; smooth, brown gray at maturity, terminating, like all oaks, in a cluster of leaf buds.

WINTER LEAF BUDS ½ inch long, slender, brown, hairy, and sharply pointed.

LEAVES Narrow, simple, alternate, 4–5 inches long, 1 to 1 ½ inches wide, with the sharply serrated, sawtooth margin terminating in bristle tips at the end of each vein. Glossy, dark green leaves in summer; yellow turning golden brown in autumn. Similar to other oaks, these trees hold onto brown, papery leaves throughout winter.

FLOWERS Beautiful 3- to 4-inch-long, yellowish-green hanging male catkins can be seen alongside leaves as they emerge in spring. Tiny female flowers produce acorns.

FRUIT Produces abundant acorns by an early age. These acorns are extraordinary looking, with cap made of fringed, hairlike scales covering half the 1-inch-long nut. They mature in two years.

HABITAT Adapts to most soils.

ECOLOGICAL VALUE Although abundant, these acorns are bitter and are eaten by squirrels, wild turkeys, blue jays, and other wildlife, only after sweet, native acorns are eaten. The leaves that remain in winter, though dried and thin, provide some shelter for wildlife.

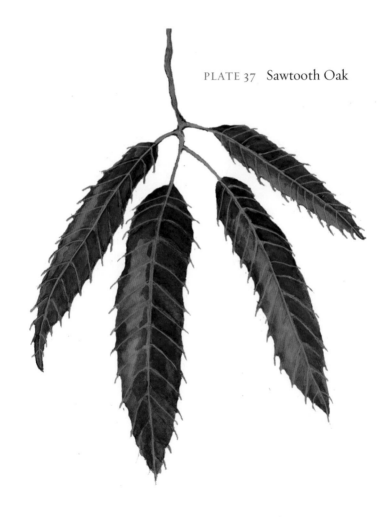

PLATE 37   Sawtooth Oak

Sawtooth oak tree covered in yellow green male catkins in spring

Frill-capped acorns of the sawtooth oak

A February storm covers sawtooth oak leaves with snow

Fissured gray bark of the sawtooth oak tree

SWAMP WHITE OAK: *Quercus bicolor*

WHERE TO SEE
Bronx: 24 Fordham Street, City Island
Brooklyn: 1104 Ditmas Avenue, Midwood
Manhattan: 200 West 84th Street, Upper West Side
Queens: 142-33 37th Avenue, Flushing
Staten Island: Royal Oak Road and Clove Lake Park, Castleton Corners

WHAT'S IN A NAME? The species name *bicolor* refers to the leaves, which are dark green above with a silvery white underside.

HEIGHT This fast-growing oak can exceed 100 feet tall with a trunk diameter of 3 feet. Once established, it can grow a foot or more each year.

CROWN SHAPE Often irregular and round with a tall, straight trunk.

BARK Gray brown to reddish brown, with broad ridges separated by deep furrows. Bark on upper branches is scaly and peeling.

TWIGS Hairy when young; smooth, reddish brown at maturity.

WINTER LEAF BUDS ⅕ inch long with a broad base, round shape, and round tip, covered by overlapping, pale, chestnut-brown scales.

LEAVES Simple, alternate, 5–10 inches long, 2–4 inches wide, with large, round, angled teeth along the margin, broad in the middle, and tapering to a narrow base, dark green above and silvery white below, covered in hairs that make the underside of the leaf feel velvety.

FLOWERS 3–4 inches long, yellowish-green hanging male catkins can be seen alongside leaves as they emerge in spring. Small female flowers produce acorns.

FRUIT Pairs of acorns attached to long, thin stalks (1–4 inches long). These 1-inch-long acorns are widest near the base, with a deep, saucer-shaped cup, enclosing one-fourth of the acorn.

HABITAT Tolerates poorly drained soil.

ECOLOGICAL VALUE The sweet, edible acorns are a favorite food for ducks, squirrels, woodpeckers, mice, rats, voles, and wild turkeys. A long-lived tree, swamp white oaks can last 350 years. Four hundred of them were planted at the World Trade Center site in late summer 2010 to honor those killed on September 11, 2001.

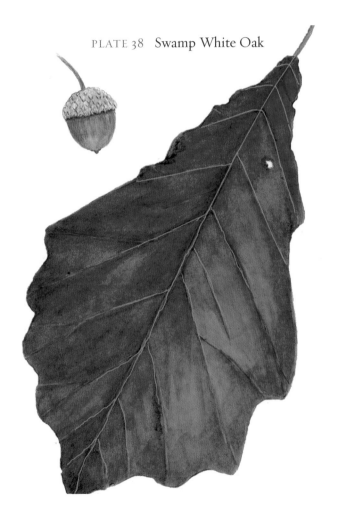

PLATE 38   Swamp White Oak

Swamp white oaks are long-lived trees. Hundreds have been planted at the World Trade Center as part of a living memorial

Broad ridges of the swamp white oak bark

Rounded lobes of the swamp white oak leaf

WILLOW OAK: *Quercus phellos*

WHERE TO SEE
Bronx: 3329 Perry Avenue, Norwood
Brooklyn: 2816 Mermaid Avenue, Coney Island
Manhattan: 305 East 7th Street, Lower East Side
Queens: Northern Boulevard between Bowne Street and Union, Flushing
Staten Island: 750 Page Avenue, Tottenville

WHAT'S IN A NAME? This tree bears willow-shaped leaves.

HEIGHT A rapidly growing oak, attaining 90 feet and, occasionally, 115 feet; trunk diameter up to 4 feet.

CROWN SHAPE Young street trees have a cone-shaped crown, while more mature trees with room to spread have a rounded crown.

BARK Smooth on young trees; rough, irregular ridges and furrows on older trees.

TWIGS Reddish or grayish brown.

WINTER LEAF BUDS Small ⅒ to ⅕ inch long, oval, pointed, and covered with reddish-brown scales. Terminal buds larger than lateral buds.

LEAVES Simple, alternate, 2–5 inches long, ½ to 1 inch wide, narrow, willow-like, tapering at both ends, shiny, pale green above, pale and dull below, with entire margins (no teeth) and a bristle tip. Leaf stems are short and wide.

FLOWERS Hanging male catkins are slender and hairy, 2–3 inches long. Tiny female flowers clustered in junctions between leaves and stems.

FRUIT Acorns are small, broad, and round with saucer-shaped cup enclosing only one-fourth of the nut and, like all members of the red oak family, require two years to mature.

HABITAT A common New York City street tree, the city is the northern edge of the willow oak's range, which stretches down to Florida and south from Illinois to Texas. This tree does well in poorly drained soil.

ECOLOGICAL VALUE An important shade tree, the willow oak's acorns provide food for squirrels, songbirds, and the occasional foraging wild turkey.

PLATE 39   Willow Oak

Willow oak on the corner of Broadway and West 78th Street

Narrow leaves and male catkins emerge in early spring

Willow oak acorns litter the ground in early September

Ridged bark of the willow oak

SWEETGUM: *Liquidambar styraciflua*

WHERE TO SEE
Bronx: 173 Ditmars Street, City Island
Brooklyn: 623 Cortelyou Road, Kensington
Manhattan: 340 Haven Avenue, Washington Heights
Queens: 157-18 Oak Avenue, Flushing
Staten Island: Jewett Avenue between Richmond Terrace and Castleton, Port Richmond

WHAT'S IN A NAME? With chewy, sweet sap, this tree has the perfect species name, *styraciflua,* which means "flowing with gum."

HEIGHT A fast grower that can attain a height of well over 100 feet.

CROWN SHAPE Pyramidal-shaped crown.

BARK The dark-gray bark becomes scaly and deeply furrowed as the tree matures. Ascending branches are a lovely silvery gray.

TWIGS As the tree matures, the twigs often have corky ridges, giving them a winged appearance.

WINTER LEAF BUDS Small, shiny with a varnished look.

LEAVES Alternate, finely toothed, aromatic, star-shaped with five to seven lobes, turning glorious shades of red, orange, yellow, and purple in autumn.

FLOWERS The reddish-green upright, pyramidal male and round, green, suspended female flowers emerge with the leaves. After pollination, male flowers fall to the ground in huge numbers, while female flowers remain, producing spiky seed balls.

FRUIT Single, green, spiny seed balls, which turn brown in autumn, hang suspended from long stems and remain long after leaves fall, giving them an ornamental look.

HABITAT Moist, well-drained soils but tolerates urban conditions very well.

ECOLOGICAL VALUE Each seed ball produces tiny seeds, which are consumed by small winter songbirds such as northern juncos, tufted titmice, and white-throated sparrows. In autumn, the star-shaped leaves are some of the most beautiful foliage in the city. Sweetgum is one of the two main types of trees that are part of the September 11 memorial at Ground Zero.

PLATE 40 Sweetgum

Bristly seedpods of the sweetgum tree hang suspended on long stalks

Male flowers of the sweetgum litter the
ground after pollination is complete

| DECIDUOUS BROADLEAF: SIMPLE, LOBED

In autumn, sweetgum leaves turn every shade of red, orange, gold, and purple

In winter, brown sweetgum seed balls fall to the ground in abundance

TULIPTREE: *Liriodendron tulipifera*

WHERE TO SEE
Bronx: Across from 955 Walton Avenue, Mt. Eden
Brooklyn: Across from 580 East 17th Street, Midwood
Manhattan: 131 Avenue B, Lower East Side
Queens: 40 Olive Place, Forest Hills Gardens
Staten Island: 75 Fort Place, St. George

WHAT'S IN A NAME? Unrelated to tulips, this tree has tulip-like flowers.

HEIGHT New York City's tallest tree, growing to a height of 150 feet. The trunk is straight and sheds its lower branches as it grows.

CROWN Broad, conical shape.

BARK Smooth, greenish gray on young trees; grayish brown with deep furrows and rounded ridges on mature trees.

TWIGS Stout, brittle, reddish brown to gray.

WINTER LEAF BUDS Dark red, flat, rounded at the tips.

LEAVES Distinctive squarish shape with four lobes and a notch between the top two lobes; 3–5 inches long and often as broad; bright green above, pale green below, turning bright yellow in fall.

FLOWERS The showy flowers have yellow-green petals splashed with orange, multiple yellow stamens, and thick yellow green pistils in the center.

FRUIT Pistils produce stout green, cone-shaped fruit that matures into dried, brown fruit made up of numerous samaras (winged seeds).

HABITAT Does well in drained or moist soils.

ECOLOGICAL VALUE Native people, pioneers, and early colonists made dugout canoes from the tall, straight trunks. Tuliptree flowers are a source of nectar for bees. In autumn, squirrels, purple finches, cardinals, and grosbeaks consume the seeds and white-tailed deer browse the twigs.

PLATE 41 Tuliptree

Notched top of the tuliptree leaf

Tuliptrees start producing flowers by the age of 20 and can continue for 200 years. Flies, beetles, honeybees, and bumblebees pollinate tuliptree flowers

Tuliptree fruit, hidden here among the leaves, are composed of samaras that separate when the fruit falls to the ground

The tuliptree trunk is straight and tall

TREE OF HEAVEN: *Ailanthus altissima*

WHERE TO SEE
Bronx: 382 Grand Concourse, Concourse Village
Brooklyn: 505 Clinton Street, Carroll Gardens
Manhattan: 23 Fort Washington Avenue, Washington Heights
Queens: 47-08 156th Street, Flushing
Staten Island: 518 Van Duzen Street, Stapleton

WHAT'S IN A NAME? Ailanthus roughly translates to "tree of heaven" and presumably refers to this tree's ability to reach toward the sky.

HEIGHT An extremely fast-growing tree—up to 10 feet in a single growing season—this tree is also short lived. It can attain a height of more than 80 feet.

CROWN SHAPE Rounded when young; open and more uneven when mature.

BARK Smooth green when young; rough, gray, and thin when mature.

TWIGS Thick, reddish brown, with velvet down and heart-shaped leaf scars; covered in lenticels (breathing pores).

WINTER LEAF BUDS Small, round, with hairy brown scales.

LEAVES Compound, alternate, feather-like, 1–3 feet long with between 11 and 41 leaflets opposite one another on a central leaf stem, ending in a single, terminal leaflet. Each leaflet is 2–6 inches long, with a narrow, pointed tip and a broad base with two or more glandular "teeth" at the base.

FLOWERS Male and female flowers are usually on separate trees. Flowers are small and greenish yellow in clusters 6–12 inches long at the tips of twigs.

FRUIT Seeds in the center of long, twisted, reddish or yellowish samaras (wings) hanging in thick clusters.

HABITAT Survives in any soil type and any urban condition.

ECOLOGICAL VALUE This tree grows and thrives where most plant life cannot, which explains why it was chosen for Betty Smith's *A Tree Grows in Brooklyn,* a beloved novel from the 1940s about a girl who is inspired by this tree's ability to survive city life.

PLATE 42   Tree of Heaven

Giant tree of heaven on the Grand Concourse in the Bronx

Immature, green samaras of the tree of heaven

Lacy compound leaves and fruit

Brown, mature samaras in late summer

GREEN ASH: *Fraxinus pennsylvanica*

WHERE TO SEE
Bronx: 150 Bowne Street, City Island
Brooklyn: 1501 Newkirk Avenue, Midwood
Manhattan: Southwest Corner West 79th Street and West End Avenue,
Upper West Side
Queens: 160-10 Laburnum Avenue, Flushing
Staten Island: 100 Belmont Place, St. George

WHAT'S IN A NAME? This tree has leaves that are distinctively green above and below.

HEIGHT A fast-growing tree, attaining a height of 70 feet.

CROWN SHAPE Irregular to round.

BARK Grayish brown with interlacing ridges creating diamond-shaped furrows.

TWIGS Slender, gray to greenish brown; leaf scars (characteristic of green ash but not white ash) semicircular to flat across the top with two lateral buds sitting on top of leaf scar (not in the notch as with white ash).

WINTER LEAF BUDS Tiny, ⅕ inch long, broad base with rounded tip and covered with three pairs of reddish-brown, overlapping scales.

LEAVES Opposite, pinnately compound with seven to nine serrated leaflets. Each leaf is 6–9 inches long, green above and green and hairless below.

FLOWERS Male and female flowers on separate trees have no petals; female flowers are suspended in loose panicles; males in tight clusters. Flowers appear after leaves emerge.

FRUIT Clusters of slender, single samaras, with broad middle and often notched tips. The narrow seed lies at the base. Maturing in fall, seeds are wind dispersed, falling close to the parent tree.

HABITAT Because of an extensive root system, green ash tolerates all kinds of soils, drought, and occasional flooding.

ECOLOGICAL VALUE Fruit consumed by woodchucks, wild turkey, cardinals, finches, squirrels, and other small rodents. Native Americans used green ash wood for their bows and green ash twigs for arrow shafts. This tree is sacred to some tribes. Unfortunately, green ash trees are under attack from a nonnative insect: the emerald ash borer (see plate 44, inset), which lays its eggs in the bark. The larvae then burrow into the wood and feed on the internal tissues of the tree, killing it within two years.

PLATE 43   Green Ash

Large green ash tree with a full crown in City Island, the Bronx

Compound leaf and flowers of the green ash tree

Clusters of green ash samaras contain narrow seeds at their base

Immature green ash bark

WHITE ASH: *Fraxinus americana*

Bronx: 170 Ditmars Street, City Island
Brooklyn: 563 Westminster Road, Midwood
Manhattan: 170 West 77th Street, Upper West Side
Queens: 31-75 29th Street, Astoria
Staten Island: 176 Locust Avenue, Grant City

WHAT'S IN A NAME? The underside of the leaf is somewhat whitish.

HEIGHT Slow-growing tree, attaining a height of more than 100 feet.

CROWN SHAPE Varies widely: pyramidal to round.

BARK Dark grayish brown with deeply interlacing ridges creating diamond-shaped furrows.

TWIGS Thick, dark green, and slightly hairy when young, maturing to a pale orange and then smooth and gray with age. Leaf scars notched at the top with winter buds sitting in the notch.

WINTER LEAF BUDS A bit longer than on the green ash: ⅗ inch long, egg shaped, blunt, rounded tip, and covered with overlapping reddish-brown, hairy scales.

LEAVES Pinnately compound with five to nine leaflets, shallow, rounded teeth to almost entire margins; papery, dark green, smooth above, whitish and smooth to slightly hairy below; leaves are opposite, 6–9 inches long.

FLOWERS No petals—male and female flowers on separate trees; female flowers are suspended in elongated clusters; males in tight clusters. Flowers appear after leaves emerge. Male flowers usually appear each year, while female flowers appear in abundance every two or three years.

FRUIT Suspended in dense clusters of slender, single samaras, broad middle and often a notched tip; with narrow seed at the base; maturing in fall; wind dispersed close to the parent tree.

HABITAT Tolerates all kinds of soils, drought, and occasional flooding.

ECOLOGICAL VALUE Fruit consumed by small mammals, song birds and ground birds. Many professional baseball players have bats made from ashwood. White ash, like green ash trees, are being devastated by the emerald ash borer (see plate 44, inset).

PLATE 44 White Ash

White ash tree with rounded crown in Midwood, Brooklyn

White ash samaras maturing during summer

Mature white ash bark, with narrow diamond-shaped furrows

BLACK LOCUST: *Robinia pseudoacacia*

WHERE TO SEE
Bronx: Grand Concourse between 162nd and 163rd Streets, Concourse
Brooklyn: 400 block of State Street, Boerum Hill
Manhattan: 518 West 111th Street, Upper West Side
Queens: 108-23 Ascan Avenue, Forest Hills Gardens
Staten Island: 1476 Richmond Road, Old Town

WHAT'S IN A NAME? The name *locust* was applied by early Christian immigrants to America who thought the trees looked like the carob tree. The carob tree has pods that somewhat resemble locusts, and some Christians believed that John the Baptist ate these pods in the wilderness.

HEIGHT A fast grower, black locusts can attain a height of 60 feet.

CROWN SHAPE Irregular outline and fairly straight trunk with thick branches arching upward.

BARK Thick, brown, deeply ridged and furrowed, with a woven, crisscrossed appearance.

TWIGS Smooth, slender, reddish brown, bearing small thorns where leaves emerge, particularly on young branches.

WINTER LEAF BUDS Tiny, in clusters of three or four, covered by overlapping scales.

LEAVES Alternate, feather/pinnate compound, 8–14 inches long, with 7–19 dark green leaflets alongside the midrib. Each leaflet 1 ½ to 2 inches long and ovate.

FLOWERS Lovely, fragrant, white hanging clusters, 4–5 inches long. Each flower is five lobed, pea shaped, with a yellow spot on the upper petals.

FRUIT Brown, flat, slender pods, 2 to 3 ½ inches long, containing four to eight dark seeds.

HABITAT Grows well in moist soils but also thrives in urban soils.

ECOLOGICAL VALUE Homesteaders planted black locust trees away from their houses to act as "lightning rods." A tree expert confirmed that in a storm, rain runs down the deep furrows of the black locust tree bark and the water attracts lightning. Squirrels feed on the seeds and the flowers are favorites of bees. The bark is so beautiful that branches and trunks of fallen trees are used to build ornamental fences, benches, and arbors in city parks. In an early snowstorm in the fall of 1985, thousands of black locusts fell, their leaves and branches heavy with snow.

PLATE 45   Black Locust

Very old black locust trunk and branches on the Lower East Side of Manhattan

Fragrant clusters of pea-like black locust flowers hang suspended in spring

Black locust seedpods contain
four to eight seeds within

Black locust bark and
lacy compound leaves

HONEY LOCUST: *Gleditsia triacanthos*

WHERE TO SEE
Bronx: 162 Ditmars Street, City Island
Brooklyn: 550 Argyle Road, Midwood
Manhattan: 250 West 157th Street, Washington Heights
Queens: 25-14 31st Street, Astoria
Staten Island: 111 Monroe Avenue, Tompkinsville

WHAT'S IN A NAME? Named for its sweet pulp, which can be fermented into beer. *Gleditsia* is named for Johann Gottlieb Gleditsch, the eighteenth-century director of the Berlin Botanic Gardens.

HEIGHT A large, fast-growing tree that can attain a height of 100 feet.

CROWN SHAPE Open, broad, and irregular, often flattened crown and large, spreading branches.

BARK Dark grayish brown, rough fissures and long, scaly ridges. In places, the bark is covered with 8-inch-long, sharp, branched spines. One can sometimes see even longer spines, as honey locust spines are modified branches and may sprout leaves. It is thought that these spines evolved to protect the tree against the large animals of the Pleistocene era.

TWIGS Thick, brown, shiny, and zigzagged, often with large spines.

WINTER LEAF BUDS Minute, lateral buds. There are no terminal buds.

LEAVES Alternate, once or twice compound (pinnately and bipinnately compound), feathery, up to 8 inches long with 7–15 pairs of opposite, narrow leaflets on each leaf. Leaves are lime green when they first open and turn dark green as they grow. Honey locust leaves are among the last leaves to emerge in the spring and among the first to fall off in autumn. They turn a brilliant gold in early fall.

FLOWERS Separate male and female flowers are on the same tree. Male flowers are in elongated clusters, and the female flowers are in slender clusters. They are quite fragrant in April or May and attract many pollinators. Female flowers produce the fruit, which start as tiny white pods.

FRUIT The flattened seedpods grow to be 6–18 inches long and turn green in summer and a dark brown, sometimes corkscrew shape in autumn when they begin to fall off the tree. The pod is filled with a sweet pulp that protects the small, hard, shiny brown seeds that resemble coffee beans.

HABITAT Another city-tough tree that can survive compacted soil, drought, salt, and heat.

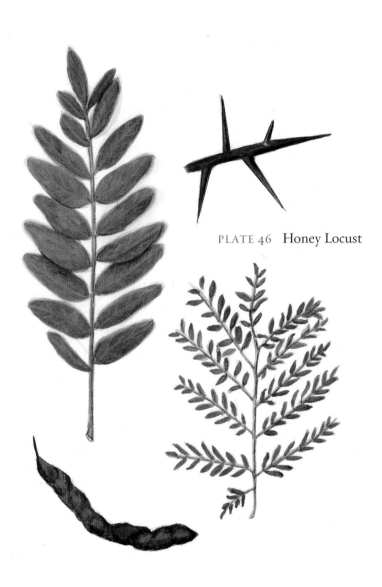

PLATE 46   Honey Locust

ECOLOGICAL VALUE   The sweet pulp of the fruit and the seeds within provide food for squirrels, birds, and other city animals.

Brilliant, lime green honey locust leaves are the last tree leaves to emerge in spring

These tiny, golden flowers are extremely fragrant. They are easily overlooked and leave you wondering where that heady scent is coming from

The curly seedpods mature in autumn

Each seedpod is filled with brown seeds that look like coffee beans

GOLDENRAIN TREE: *Koelreuteria paniculata*

WHERE TO SEE
Bronx: On the median at East 164th and Grand Concourse,
Concourse Village
Brooklyn: 605 Washington Avenue, Prospect Heights
Manhattan: 70 West 91st Street, Upper West Side
Queens: 29-08 31st Street, Astoria
Staten Island: Westervelt Avenue between Crescent and Layton Avenues,
New Brighton

WHAT'S IN A NAME? The falling golden-yellow flowers inspired the common
name *goldenrain*.

HEIGHT This small to medium-sized tree grows to 20–40 feet.

CROWN SHAPE Full, round, spreading crown, almost as wide as it is tall.

BARK Gray brown, with orange inner bark; furrowed with age.

TWIGS Light brown, zigzagged with prominent leaf scars and lenticels
(breathing pores).

WINTER BUDS Small, lateral buds next to leaf scar.

LEAVES Beautiful, alternate, compound, with up to 15 leaflets. Dark green
with yellow-green midveins; the leaflets have wavy teeth along the margins.

FLOWERS Bright-yellow petals with orange center fold back and expose bold
stamens with yellow filaments and reddish-brown anthers. Flowers
are arranged in foot-long terminal panicles.

FRUIT The flower ovaries turn into lantern-shaped, papery seedpods,
which are pale green at first, turning pink in fall and brown in winter,
where they can remain suspended from the tree. The black seeds within
are easily germinated.

HABITAT This little tree does well in urban environments and is tolerant of
different soil types and air pollution.

ECOLOGICAL VALUE Brought to Europe from Asia in the 1740s, the
goldenrain tree was introduced to America in 1809 when Thomas Jefferson
received seeds from a fellow plant lover in France. The long-lasting, profuse
flowers attract pollinators. The broad crown provides shade.

PLATE 47   Goldenrain Tree

Goldenrain tree on the corner of West 91st Street and Columbus Avenue, Manhattan

Ornamental trunk of the goldenrain tree

Golden flowers with orange centers fall like rain in the autumn,
giving the tree its name

The lantern-like seedpods mature in fall

JAPANESE PAGODATREE, OR CHINESE SCHOLAR TREE: *Styphnolobium japonicum*

WHERE TO SEE

Bronx: Northeast Corner of River Avenue and East 164th Street, Concourse

Brooklyn: 518 Clinton Street, Carroll Gardens

Manhattan: 35 West 67th Street, Upper West Side

Queens: 30 Winter Street, Forest Hills Gardens

Staten Island: 4 Knox Place, Castleton Corners

WHAT'S IN A NAME? The genus name *Styphnolobium* means dense crown with pods, as this tree bears many pods.

HEIGHT A medium-sized tree that grows to 60 feet.

CROWN SHAPE Spreading branches form a round, symmetrical crown on young and mature trees.

BARK Grayish-brown furrows and scaly ridges.

TWIGS Dark green and smooth or with fine hairs and prominent tan lenticels (breathing pores). Twigs turn dark gray as they mature.

WINTER LEAF BUDS Small, brown.

LEAVES Alternate, pinnately compound (feather shaped), 6–10 inches long with 7–17 ovate leaflets with entire margins (no teeth); shiny, dark green above, pale with fine hairs below.

FLOWERS Tree must be at least 10 years old to bloom, but the creamy, white, pea-shaped flowers open in mid to late summer, often completely covering the tree in their showy clusters at the ends of twigs.

FRUIT 6- to 12-inch pod narrowing between the seeds, resembling a string of beads; greenish yellow at first, turning brown in autumn.

HABITAT Considered an "urban-tough" tree because of its tolerance of all types of soil, drought, and salt.

ECOLOGICAL VALUE Originally from Japan, China, and Korea, and commonly planted throughout the five boroughs. People all over the city notice these trees, as they are the last to bloom in summer in great profusion, providing both beauty and shade on hot July and August days.

PLATE 48   Japanese Pagodatree

Flowering Japanese pagodatree in the West Village, Manhattan

White, pea-like flowers litter the cars and streets in late summer

Seedpods completely cover this Japanese pagodatree in the Bronx

Seedpods are connected to one another, making them look like beads in a necklace

KENTUCKY COFFEETREE: *Gymnocladus dioicus*

WHERE TO SEE
Bronx: Grand Concourse and East 164th Street, edge of Joyce Kilmer Park, Concourse
Brooklyn: 750 Rockaway Avenue, Brownsville
Manhattan: Schwab House courtyard, West 73rd Street between West End Avenue and Riverside Drive, Upper West Side
Queens: 100-11 70th Avenue, Forest Hills
Staten Island: 1150 Clove Road, West Brighton

WHAT'S IN A NAME?   The seeds look like coffee beans, and early American colonists roasted the seeds to make a coffee substitute.

HEIGHT   Up to 70 feet, sometimes taller.

CROWN SHAPE   Oval with ascending branches spread far apart, giving the crown an open look and allowing sunlight to penetrate the soil below. Crown is irregular when tree is young, becoming more symmetrical as it matures.

BARK   Grayish brown with deep furrows and ridges that may flare along the sides, resembling the bark of the honey locust tree but more textured and highly ornamental.

TWIGS   Graying brown, stout, contorted, and highly patterned with enormous leaf scars.

WINTER LEAF BUDS   Very small lateral buds. Twigs lack terminal buds.

LEAVES   Bipinnately, twice compound, huge, up to 3 feet long and 2 feet wide, composed of pointed, blue-green leaflets with entire margins (no teeth). Leaves appear in late spring, giving the tree a "naked" appearance most of the year.

FLOWERS   They appear in late spring along with the new leaves. There are male and female flowers on different trees. Male flowers appear in 4-inch-long dense clusters. Fragrant female flowers are in 1-foot-long clusters.

FRUIT   Female flowers produce large, thick, pale-green fruit pods that become hard and brown in autumn and may continue to hang from the tree into the following spring. Each pod contains several round brown seeds that resemble coffee beans.

HABITAT   Adapts well to different soils. Though native to wet, rich soil, this tree tolerates poor, dry urban soils.

PLATE 49   Kentucky Coffeetree

ECOLOGICAL VALUE The leaves and seeds, when eaten raw, are poisonous. Like the locust trees and redbud tree, this tree is a legume that bears nitrogen-fixing bacteria in its roots. These important microbes "fix" much-needed nitrogen from the atmosphere into the soil. Other plants are then able to take the nitrogen up through their roots. This tree is ornamental in every season.

Large Kentucky coffeetree at the edge of Joyce Kilmer Park
and the Grand Concourse in the Bronx

Bipinnately compound Kentucky coffeetree
leaves can be more than 3 feet long

Kentucky coffeetree leaves turning
color in autumn

HORSE CHESTNUT: *Aesculus hippocastanum*

WHERE TO SEE

Bronx: 573 Minnieford Avenue, City Island
Brooklyn: 1207 Ditmas Avenue, Midwood
Manhattan: 4 Hamilton Terrace, Hamilton Heights
Queens: Median opposite 43 Greenway Terrace, Forest Hills Gardens
Staten Island: 204 Victory Boulevard, Tompkinsville

WHAT'S IN A NAME? The species name *hippocastanum* translates to horse chestnut, as horses, not humans, can eat the nuts.

HEIGHT A large tree, the horse chestnut can attain a height of 85 feet.

CROWN SHAPE A towering tree with widely spreading branches and large, straight trunk creating a huge bell-like shape. The sweeping branches dip up, then down, then up again, making the entire tree look like a giant candelabra.

BARK The mature scaly bark is grayish brown and broken into shallow fissures.

TWIGS Pale brown, thick, ending in large, sticky terminal leaf bud.

WINTER LEAF BUDS Large, covered with a sticky resin, which binds the bud scales together and protects the leaf within from winter's cold and wind. In early spring, the warmth of the sun melts this resin and the bud scales are able to open.

LEAVES Large, opposite leaves are palmately compound with five to seven leaflets, which all emerge at once from the bud. Each leaflet can be up to 10 inches long. The leaf stem alone can be up to 7 inches, and when it falls off the twig, it leaves a large leaf scar in the shape of a horse's hoof.

FLOWERS Flower clusters are white, speckled with red or yellow, which are nectar guidelines for pollinators. These clusters appear on erect spikes giving the flowers the look of white flames atop an enormous candelabra: the flowers of the horse chestnut are known as *candles*.

FRUIT The flowers produce spiny seedpods encasing a hard, shiny brown nut, which looks like a chestnut but is not. The pod, a large green husk protected with short, sharp spines, splits into three parts when it falls to the ground, freeing the nut inside. The nuts, called *conkers*, are poisonous to humans but not to most other mammals.

HABITAT A hardy city tree used for beauty and shade in all the great cities of the world.

PLATE 50   Horse Chestnut

ECOLOGICAL VALUE Squirrels feed on and bury the nuts. Butterflies, bumblebees, and other insects are attracted to the honey-like scent of the flowers.

Mature bark of the horse chestnut tree

Palmate compound leaves are made of five to seven leaflets and are arranged opposite one another other on the branch

After the flowers are pollinated, the yellow spots turn red

Horse chestnuts are spiky and cover a hard, shiny, brown nut

TREE
PEOPLE

Interviews with New Yorkers who volunteer their time caring for our city trees led me to the key people and organizations professionally responsible for the planting and welfare of our street trees. I asked the following people about their role in making our city green. These influential and inspirational people reveal much about the city's love affair with our leafy neighbors.

Nina Bassuk

CORNELL UNIVERSITY

Nina is a professor and program leader of the Urban Horticulture Institute at Cornell University and author of *Trees in the Urban Landscape*. She invented the substance Structural Soil and created many tree care practices used today by urban arborists and organizations that plant and care for New York City's street trees and for trees in urban areas throughout the United States. I called her in Ithaca, New York, and we talked about her childhood connection to nature.

"I grew up in Flatbush, Brooklyn, in Midwood, on 28th between Avenue J and Avenue K. There was no one in my family who was green. I remember looking in the 'Arts and Leisure' section of the *New York Times* and seeing seed catalogs. I was eight or nine years old and sent away for the catalogs. I would read them and look at vegetables and flowers, and I got more and more catalogs. Then I bought fluorescent lights and started to grow things. I tried to propagate sweet potatoes, avocados, and carrots in our kitchen. I just tried to grow everything from the fridge and from the catalogs. I went through different phases: miniature roses, African violets, potatoes, pumpkins in a pot."

In junior high school, Nina figured out five different ways to propagate plants, which won her a science fair prize.

She recalled, "I was almost embarrassed because this was just something I loved to do. I love to grow things. We had a postage stamp garden with a Norway maple in front of the house. I liked the tree, and I liked trying to grow things in the city. Making an area bloom and come to life was very powerful for me." After graduating from Cornell, Nina went on to graduate school in England and worked on propagating woody plants and "then, when I was looking for a job after my PhD, this new program started at Cornell University in urban horticulture. My old idea of greening over the city and making it bloom was something that appealed to me. In 1980, I started working there. There hadn't been an urban horticulture program before that. It grew out of the sprouting of urban gardens: community gardens in the South Bronx and growing vegetables in vacant lots on the Lower East Side." She then said something profound: "This was the most democratic thing I could do." She wanted to figure out "how to get these trees to grow on the street in these little boxes and concrete. This would do something for everyone: for all the people who walk down city streets. This is where I wanted to put my efforts."

I asked Nina about her invention: Structural Soil. "Structural Soil grew out of the question, 'How are we going to grow plants out of the sidewalks?' Once you prepare the ground for a sidewalk, you compact it so much it stops root growth. How do you make room for the roots? How much soil do you need to allow a tree to grow to its envisioned size? The roadblock was that the soil would need to bear the load of the pavement. Can we develop a soil that can be compacted to meet the engineers' design for road bearing? We experimented with how much soil and matrix was needed. Structural Soil is part rigid matrix and part soil: you can land an airplane on it."

Nina developed a specification sheet for MillionTreesNYC for new tree planting: a written document spelling out the standard of quality that these trees must meet.

Nina posed and answered the critical question, "How is the tree grown so it's going to be a really good tree? The whole idea of open trenches and not compacting the soil provide simple answers: the more usable the soil volume, the better the tree will be."

Nina continues to stay involved with the city. She gives workshops for the botanical gardens, and the New York City Parks Department. It is indeed fortunate for us that Nina grew up in Brooklyn, and still cares about the trees and people of this city.

Adrian Benepe
NEW YORK CITY DEPARTMENT OF PARKS AND RECREATION

The first thing I noticed when I walked into Commissioner Adrian Benepe's office in the Central Park Armory were the treetops. He had a great view of the Central Park Zoo and all the nature within and around it. The office was abuzz with activity, so I got straight to the point and asked him about his experience with New Yorkers and their trees.

"I honestly think that New Yorkers care more about trees than people in any other city," he boasted.

"Why do you think that?" I asked and listened while he enthusiastically rolled out his unrehearsed answer.

"Trees are so important in a city like this. New York is so densely populated, with such big buildings, and you feel so overwhelmed. People just love the trees: the shade they provide, the types of birds that sit in them in the morning and in the evening, the color they bring to a block, and the way they make the block feel better. It's not coincidental that during the bad days of the 1960s and

'70s when block associations were being formed to stop the hemorrhaging of people from neighborhoods and to preserve the quality of life, that one of the first things most block associations did was plant trees. When you look at what was the founding purpose of most block associations it was to plant trees. Although the city is now planting the trees, one of the essential activities of many block associations and civic organizations is to care for their trees. Trees are an essential civic activity.

"Today tree planting and tree care have become part of the city's major policy initiative through PlaNYC, and the MillionTreesNYC initiative. We have here in the city of New York, one of the finest urban trees programs in the country. We have a very sophisticated program within the Parks Department of tree planting and tree care [and] a little less tree care now with the fiscal crisis."

Then the commissioner talked about his scientific understanding of what trees actually do for us. "The MillionTrees program is based on research done by the U.S. Forest Service's study that has quantified the financial benefits of street trees in terms of mitigating pollution, taking up storm-water runoff, increasing property values, and reducing the heat-island effect," he said. "They came up with a formula that, for every dollar the city spends on planting and maintaining street trees, there's a return of about $5.50. That was enormously helpful in persuading the mayor to launch MillionTreesNYC and to invest hundreds of millions of dollars into a tree program with a scientific underpinning by the U.S. Forest Service. This paved the way for the formal relationship between the U.S. Forest Service and the city, and, in fact, the Forest Service, through the Department of Agriculture, gave us a $2 million grant to help launch and sustain the MillionTreesNYC Training Program, which is a training program for young adults in various jobs that relate to tree care and greening the city of New York."

Commissioner Benepe then pointed out that not everyone loves trees. "As many people as there are who love trees, there are homeowners who write letters saying how much agony and pain trees cause in their lives. The leaves end up in their gutter, 'Please, please, please cut down the tree.' We always send them a letter that points out all of the blessings brought to us by trees. Raking leaves and cleaning out gutters is a small thank you we can give a tree for all of the benefits that they provide us: cooling our homes, cleaning our air, taking up storm water. One of the things we no longer do is get homeowners' permission to plant a street tree near their house. We wouldn't ask the homeowner for permission to put in a fire hydrant or a bus stop or a parking sign. Trees are part of the city's infrastructure. They perform a very valuable service at a very low cost."

When I asked the commissioner what he would like New Yorkers to know about their trees, he said, "We want to promote the scientific value of trees: they take in our waste product, carbon dioxide, and turn out oxygen for us. I think one thing people don't know is that some trees are better than others in terms of pollution. The London plane tree is probably the very best tree in terms of fighting pollution. It has very large leaves with large surface areas that absorb more particulate matter and more carbon dioxide and give off more oxygen than any other tree."

Sam Bishop

TREES NEW YORK

In the 1970s, many New Yorkers were concerned because the Parks Department's budget for tree care had been cut substantially. Several groups offered to work on a volunteer basis to care for the city's trees. Over time, these groups became known as the New York City Street Tree Consortium, later evolving into Trees New York. Sam Bishop, an attorney, is Director of Education for Trees New York. His love of trees brought him to this organization. Sam explained, "Our mission is to plant, preserve, protect, and care for New York City's urban forest. And that's not just our street trees, but all the plants and animals that go along with the trees. I'm sure you know that the more science and research we do, it's very difficult to pick out one part of the environment and attempt to isolate it and care for that thing successfully. You can't talk about the trees unless you're talking about the animals that use them for habitat, the insects that feed on them, and the animals that feed on those insects."

In caring for the city's trees, he said, "you also have to take into consideration the city's infrastructure—our buildings, sidewalks, underground pipes, gas lines, and long-term planning, always with this question in mind: Are we doing things that benefit trees? For example, when planning a new sidewalk or putting up a new building, if developers consult a landscape architect or urban arborist, they would encourage the developer to prepare the ground for trees by using one of two systems that help the soil. One system is Structural Soil and the other is the Silva Cell Tree and Stormwater Management System. Developers are encouraged to use these wherever they build in order to help tree roots grow through the soil."

A large part of Trees New York's mission is getting the public engaged. As Sam puts it, they want city residents "caring for the city's urban forest." Sam lit up when he talked about the citizen pruner program: a 12-hour training program that licenses people to care for and prune the city's trees. "We train them to cut away dead branches, and if you're not licensed and you do this, it's a thousand dollar fine when you cut something off a tree. The focus has always been on caring for newly planted trees: the first couple of years after the tree is planted, when they're smallest and most vulnerable. When they come from the nursery, they've lost over 90% of their roots. At the time that they pull the trees out of the ground, they cut off almost all of their roots, which means that they've lost most of their ability to take up water. That is why you need to baby them for that period. Typically, a tree's roots will reach as far away from the trunk as the tree is tall. So if you put a tree in that's 15 feet tall, when it was in the nursery and happy, it had roots that extended 15 feet out from the trunk in all directions. When they cut that root ball, they're probably cutting a 30-inch root ball. Now you've gone from 15 feet on a side to 15 inches on a side."

Sam has such a passion for trees. Whenever he sees grates around trees he knows the tree will be gravely injured. "Grates kill trees," Sam said with feeling, "and it's costly and complicated to have the grates removed to save the trees. Now Parks is trying to do everything they can to discourage grates. The urban foresters have done a really good job in demanding that the tree pits get cut as big as possible."

I asked Sam what was the most important message he could send to New Yorkers. "It is to be actively involved with your trees. Plant flowers in the tree beds, and water them. The word gets around in the neighborhood. People really do appreciate what you do for trees." He told a story about a recent experience. "I was out watering trees last Saturday and a woman yelled from the other side of the street, 'Oh thank you for doing that. There's this older man who usually waters the trees here.' And I yelled back across First Avenue, 'Yeah, that's my dad.'" Sam's father has been caring for trees for many decades and inspired his son to love trees. Sam Bishop Sr. told me that in the mid 1980s, First Avenue, between 14th and 20th streets, had empty tree pits or dying trees. Sam Sr. created a survey of all the tree pits and photographed them. He sent the survey into the Parks Department and got them to start to plant trees in the empty pits. He was then asked to join the New York City Street Tree Consortium, which he has been part of since 1987, and which he is now president of. Twenty-five years ago, during hot, dry summers after work, he would take his two children, fill a bucket with water, and go out and water the parched trees. As with so many of the tree activists we have interviewed for this book, the love of trees is passed on from generation to generation.

Wayne Cahilly

NEW YORK BOTANICAL GARDEN

Wayne Cahilly has been at the New York Botanical Garden since 1982. I don't know anyone who has more knowledge about trees than Wayne. He is a fount of information. His knowledge is encyclopedic, and no one likes to talk about trees more than Wayne. Ask him a single question, and 20 minutes later, he is still answering it, going into deeper and deeper layers of science, culture, and history. I asked Wayne to talk about what a young city tree is up against and what it needs.

Wayne took a breath and walked me through it. "If you take the diameter of the tree in inches, 6 inches above the root ball, it's going to take about that many years from the transplanting event for the tree to be somewhat established. If it's a 2-inch caliper tree, it's going to take two years for that tree to establish itself, provided you've given it your best efforts: you've watered it, made sure it didn't suffer from drought. You didn't excessively prune it when you planted it. You let it go through a cycle and then you prune what it doesn't need. And you've planted it in an adequate location to begin with. You know, site selection is a big, big deal. You have to put trees in places that are hospitable to the species, where they are genetically capable of dealing with the circumstances. The city planting locations are more like floodplains. Sycamores, honey locusts, sweetgums are all floodplain species. You have soil that is compacted and otherwise dense and devoid of oxygen. Trees' roots take in oxygen from the soil and give off CO_2 and other gasses (the opposite of leaves). So when you have roots that are going through the normal life cycle, they're taking in the amount of oxygen that that species needs.

"If you put a tree in a tree pit and you backfill with whatever soil came out of the hole and amend it at the time, it will eventually become low in organic material because organic material breaks down. And the end result is you have a soil, which structurally is indisposed to having water and oxygen being a part of it. Trucks going by on all the streets, and the subway underneath, all make the soil settle. Stand on the street, close your eyes, stick your fingers in your ears, and just feel what is going on around you. All the fine soil particles over time vibrate down into the open space. Soil becomes monolithic, no matter what it was when you put it in the hole when you planted the tree. As time goes forward from planting, that soil becomes more like bottomland soil from the perspective of the root: it's dense, devoid of oxygen, and doesn't wet or dry easily."

Wayne then talked about the effect of road salt on city trees. "Desiccation is a problem because we use so much road salt," he said. "Salt can be flushed from trees by rainwater, which will bind the salt. But sodium and chloride ions can't be metabolized by a tree, so they'll end up at the tips of everything, causing marginal leaf burn and bud damage. After a really salty winter you'll see that the terminal buds on twigs won't leaf out. Three or four inches back, side buds will break. What's happened is all the salt has ended up out there at the leaf buds and desiccates the leaves."

It is indeed tough being a city tree.

Jennifer Greenfeld
NEW YORK CITY DEPARTMENT OF PARKS AND RECREATION

I met Jennifer Greenfeld in the Forestry Trailer next to the Olmsted Building in Flushing Meadows Corona Park, Queens. It happened to be a day that a horde of camera crews were setting up for the U.S. Open at Arthur Ashe Stadium in the park. It's a circuitous route from the Grand Central Parkway to the park, and at one point, I was hopelessly lost and feeling anxious. I called Jennifer, and she calmly guided me back to where I needed to be. All of a sudden I was passing the eerie ruins of the World's Fair, where I worked in 1964, after my first year of college. Then I was passing the New York State Ice Skating building where I learned to ice skate when I was five. The familiar landscape calmed me and the trees in the park were spectacular. There is a lot of personal history in this park.

Jennifer warmly welcomed me at the door. The Forestry Trailer, a double wide, was actually lovely inside. Low, pale-green walls separate the workspaces, and the area is large, airy, and filled with light.

Jennifer started off by making sure I knew that MillionTreesNYC is not necessarily a program to plant a million street trees. "As we go through and fill blocks with trees, we get a better feeling for how many trees can really fit, and I suspect we can fit more than 220,000," their latest estimate. Either way, that is a lot of young trees. I asked Jennifer how things work during a drought. It had not rained in weeks.

She explained, "What I know best are the new trees. All the street trees that we plant are planted by contractors, and we require a two-year guarantee. During that time, they are required to water the trees. We have really stepped up our focus on getting the contractors to water. We talk to them even before they put trees into the ground. We have almost fifty thousand trees under guarantee from the beginning of the summer, and some of the contractors have almost 8,000 trees that they have to water. So we sit them down even before they put the trees into the ground and say to them, 'Okay, tell us how the trees are going to get watered. What size are your trucks? What tanks do you use? Where are you getting the water from? How large are your crews?'"

Jennifer is petite and bristling with purpose, energy and intelligence. I can just imagine these contractors on the hot seat. "We ask them to tell us where they're going to be ahead of time. We get phone contacts for each of the crew leaders. We've hired supervision to literally follow them. Last summer was a rainy summer, but we made them water even when it rained. Rain is no reason not to water. They would call us and say 'We look ridiculous out here. We're standing here and it's raining and you're making us water.' I would say, 'Yeah, we are. If you dig down you may not actually have much water under that tree.' The contractors have to water until the end of October because the trees are still growing."

Jennifer talked about her relationship to nature as a young person. "I grew up in Baltimore in a suburban neighborhood, which was leafy. I went camping with my family when I was little, so I liked nature. But when I spent a year in Israel, working on a farm on a kibbutz, I had a different relationship to nature. Just growing things gave me some connection to nature that I never had before. I loved that idea that we can have a role in growing things that are of benefit. Then I went to college at Penn in Philadelphia and I loved being in the city. I just started asking questions like 'What is the role of nature in cities, and how do I fit in? And why do I love being in the city? What makes it great?' And then you see that trees are the 'spokespersons' for nature in the city. They are the iconic symbol of nature in the city. Being in the city and loving biology and loving growing things, I sort of slowly narrowed my interests to urban forestry in a very specific way. My senior thesis in college was doing a street tree survey with elementary school kids near the campus. Then I went to forestry school at Yale, and in forestry school, I focused on how trees fit into the urban environment. One thing built on another, and I ended up here, which has got to be one of the best gigs for an urban forester in the country."

I asked Jennifer my standard question: What would she want New Yorkers to know about trees? She became thoughtful and quietly said that she wants people who never think about trees to notice them. "Just to see them and imagine the park or the block without them. Think how our environment and our day-to-day lives would be if there were no trees. Do you really want to have a picnic in a parking lot? You should be able to follow the trees down your street, to your playground, to your park, and then to the forests of Van Cortlandt, or Greenbelt, or Alley Pond Park."

Bill Logan
URBAN ARBORISTS

We had heard about Bill from the many people we interviewed for this book. Bill Logan is the founder and president of Urban Arborists. He teaches horticulture and winter tree identification classes at the New York Botanical Garden, where he is a member of their advisory board. On top of all that, Bill is a natural history writer. His books include *Dirt, the Ecstatic Skin of the Earth*, *Oak: The Frame of Civilization*, and he is now working on *Air*. Bill has been planting and caring for New York City street trees for a long time. Many block associations and business improvement districts hire him to care for neighborhood trees. Of his organization, Urban Arborists, he says the following. "We've tried to make New York a place that is a green city. Most of what's done that is bad to trees in New York is not done through ill will, though occasionally it is. It is mostly done through ignorance. People say, 'Oh, I have a great idea! I'm going to add more soil so my tree has more to eat.' Then they add 4 or 5 inches of soil to the tree pit and they're basically suffocating the roots so the tree declines, and they don't mean for that to happen. We've done a thing for many years with the Parks Department called 'tree rescue' during the winter. We go around the city, and if trees are growing into those metal grates and harming themselves, we carefully remove the grates. We cut the grates with a chop saw: one of those saws that they use to cut concrete. It's a little tricky because often the tree is growing over the grate. You have to tease it out without doing harm to the tree. Sometimes people leave strings of lights on the tree, and they're starting to grow into the tree, which will girdle it, so we'll remove those. Sometimes people have poured concrete right up to the tree and completely covered the tree bed. People report problems or the city tells us of problems, or we just notice things as we're driving around.

"One of the craziest things we found was somebody who had cut and poured this sheet metal enclosure that went entirely over the tree pit and then chimneyed it up the tree to a 12-foot height to protect the tree from dog pee. And then they painted the metal all black! They obviously thought this would protect the tree from any dog waste, but they were killing the poor baby; they just didn't know it! One of the things we emphasize in our work is, I go to a client and I don't just say, 'You need to do this and this.' I say, 'It looks like this is happening to your tree. I wonder why it's happening?' I'll ask them some questions: 'What's been happening around this tree?' and they'll say, 'Well, I don't think anything.' And I'll say, 'Nothing? What about this trench around the tree.' And they'll say, 'Oh, yeah! Con Ed came.' And we'll tell them that it's worse for the tree to be cut at the roots than the top. A lot of our work is fun because we get to talk about trees and think about trees and how they live and die. There's a whole subgroup of people in New York who spend their time trying to get good things happening to trees." Trudy and I agreed that this is what we have been seeing across the city, and it truly is inspirational.

David Moore

NEW YORK RESTORATION PROJECT

In 1995, Bette Midler noticed a great decline in the northern Manhattan parks. The areas that people should have been enjoying were full of trash and unfit for use. Bette decided to do something about it and founded the New York Restoration Project (NYRP). Then, in 1999, there was an opportunity to purchase and place in a land trust 55 community gardens throughout the five boroughs. So NYRP purchased the gardens and received corporate, private, and foundation donations to remodel and improve the sites. They used those gardens to create "village greens" to rally the community around but also used the gardens as platforms for environmental education, stewardship, and neighborhood meetings for community improvement.

With a successful track record, Bette and NYRP were about to enter the tree world. As part of the sustainability initiative PlaNYC 2030, Mayor Michael R. Bloomberg announced that he wanted to increase the tree canopy of the city by 25–30%. Around this time, Bette Midler held a press conference and announced that NYRP intended to plant a million trees. It all came together, and the "million tree" idea was hatched.

David Moore is the MillionTreesNYC forester for the New York Restoration Project. David is passionate about trees and the natural world. He has sparkling brown eyes, dark hair that stands straight up, and a contagious smile.

David talked about "the arena of thought around humans and their environment: the way that we think New York City is ours or the world is part of our environment. We are, in fact, a small speck in a much greater system. And ecology is a key thing to keep in mind for all aspects of life. If ecology is a study of systems, well New York City has its own ecology too. If we can keep in mind that everything here before humans was forest, it sort of changes the way you think about trees. If we can see we are all interdependent, then we might be more realistic about our expectations of the world. When people say 'I'm so mad it's raining.' I say, 'Well I'm sure glad there's water to drink and food to eat.' To think that the environment is something that we control or is something alien to us, leads to all these other confusing things. We need to think that we didn't come into the world, but we come out of the world like a leaf comes out of a tree. If the leaf appeared on the tree it would think the tree is a very confusing and scary place. But if the leaf could consider the fact that the tree made the leaf and the leaf is a part of the tree and it needs the other leaves and the branches and the stem and the roots to survive, then you start appreciating things in different ways and have a greater understanding. It's a little less frustrating than thinking that the whole environment is against you."

Karla Osorio-Pérez
BROOKLYN BOTANIC GARDEN

Karla grew up in Puerto Rico with a backyard full of trees: tamarind, coconut, oranges, and breadfruit. "I grew up composting and watching my parents gardening for food," she said. "I remember my mother going to the backyard to grab leaves to make sofrito or make whatever we needed for spices to add to the chicken or to the beans."

Karla earned a bachelor's degree in biology at the University of Puerto Rico and then traveled to El Salvador and worked for the Peace Corps, where she did environmental education and forestry programs. After El Salvador, Karla came to New York City. "I started with Brooklyn Botanic Garden as the compost instructor," she said, "and then I became the compost manager. Currently, I am the community field manager of GreenBridge, a community outreach program with the Brooklyn Botanic Garden. I work mostly with adults. The mission of GreenBridge is to educate the community. We work with leaders in the community, such as community gardeners who would like to use gardening as a tool to educate and engage others in the neighborhood or to empower others in the neighborhood to work with justice issues like food security. We are under the Education Department at the Brooklyn Botanic Garden. We promote sustainable gardening practices, which include composting, learning about native plants, and soil and water conservation."

She explained how her organization became involved with the Million-TreesNYC initiative: "GreenBridge and Brooklyn Botanic Garden have been working with street tree care for years. We developed tree care tip sheets before MillionTreesNYC started. We got together with the Department of Parks and Recreation when they started looking for organizations to partner with, to motivate the community about street tree care and stewardship. GreenBridge gives many tree care workshops to the community. The workshops are about two hours long. We talk about the benefits of trees, and I ask them why they like trees. We talk about why it is important to take care of trees and how to take care of them, which includes cultivation and aeration of the soil, picking up litter, and keeping the tree beds cleaned and watered. We get tools funded by MillionTreesNYC. I show them the tools: a cultivator, a weeder, a trowel, gloves, and a bucket. We go out to a tree, and I show them how to work with each tool and how to be careful with the roots. I explain why they need to use gloves, especially in an urban environment where dogs use the tree beds, and people throw garbage in them. Watering is a big, big thing. In the summer when we don't have a lot of rain, it's important that trees get 15 gallons of water each week. I teach them how to water correctly; how to make it so all the water goes into the bed and doesn't run onto the sidewalk. Very slowly is key. A newly planted tree should get 20 gallons of water every week."

Karla recently went to the Sunset Park Library to give the street tree care workshop and, again, MillionTreesNYC provided the tools. "After this course, I told them that they have permission from the Department of Parks and Recreation to mulch and water the tree beds. We suggest that they go to Greenwood Cemetery, which has free mulch year round. They can go with containers, plastic garbage bags, and their shovels and take as many woodchips as they need. Greenwood Cemetery is happy for the community to take the chips."

Barrett Robinson
NEW YORK RESTORATION PROJECT

Bette Midler brought in Barrett Robinson as vice president of Horticulture and Construction at the New York Restoration Project. Barrett greeted me with these words, "We want people to know all the benefits that trees provide: how they collect storm water and really help mitigate the combined sewer system we have in the city. If you get an inch of rain, all the sewer and storm water combine and dump into the rivers. Trees clean the air of particulates. The carbon dioxide and oxygen exchange that's part of photosynthesis is an important piece of what trees do. And they shade our streets and homes. Any time you can shade any surface, it cools it significantly so being able to shade the city to help with the urban heat island effect is important. In addition, for store owners and people in the community, it not only increases property values to live in a tree-lined street, but people prefer to shop in a district with trees: it's cooler; it's more pleasant and attractive. Habitat for wildlife is also important because as we build over the city you lose homes for bugs and birds and any other critters that live in our ecosystem. Developing those ecosystems is also really important."

Barrett continued, "One tree can offer so many benefits. Our infrastructure systems have regularly scheduled inspections and maintenance visits. If you took some of that money and focused on trees, they are the only infrastructure that improves over time as long as you keep them intact."

This last idea had never occurred to me, that trees are indeed part of our infrastructure, and if we protect them, they grow more important.

Eric Thomann
NEW YORK CITY COMMUNITY GARDEN COALITION

I met Eric Thomann at the beautiful Riverside Valley Community Garden, planted and cared for by Jenny Benitez and her volunteers on West 138th Street and 12th Avenue, a few blocks north of the uptown Fairway Market. Eric arrived on his bicycle, which he rode from his Brooklyn home. He is vice president of the New York City Community Garden Coalition of the Parks Department and teaches sustainable gardening with native plants in the New School as well. Eric was at the garden to lead a workshop for tree stewards, and Trudy and I were part of about a dozen people in attendance. He led us to the back of a Parks Department truck and handed out a 5-gallon bucket filled with tools we would use to help our tree. He said that we could then take all these items home with us: a pair of gloves, a dandelion weeder, a cultivator (the claw), a trowel, and leaf-litter garbage bags. MillionTreesNYC funds these workshops in partnership with the Parks Department and its private partners.

Eric gathered us in a circle and told us that once we completed this workshop we could train new tree stewards: that we weren't just 12 people, we were really 144 people. "We will leave here today with the ability to bring in a passerby or a neighbor and teach them some of the very simple methods you can do to help the trees survive," he said. "Eric asked each participant to name valuable attributes of street trees. The tree stewards-in-training developed this list:

- Trees provide shade (I was in the group sitting in the shade, and I looked over at the people sitting in the hot sun, shading their eyes with their hands.)
- Trees make everything look better.
- Trees provide habitat for wildlife.
- Trees give us oxygen.
- Trees absorb storm water runoff. Eric said, "Combined sewage overflow [CSO] is the runoff when it rains hard, and the rain runs down the street and into the sewer where it ends up in the sewage treatment plant. This puts the sewage over the top, and it runs into our rivers, harbors, and beaches. CSO can cost a lot of money. Trees absorb the water and cut down on CSO."
- Trees prevent soil erosion. Bedrock and a supply of water will make soil in about a million years. Trees prevent that soil from eroding.
- Trees increase property values.
- Trees bring people together.

Eric led us to a tree on West 138th Street. Concrete almost completely surrounded the pit. There was just enough soil to cultivate. Eric demonstrated. First, he put on his gloves to protect his hands from dog waste and bacteria. He then opened one of the garbage bags and put debris from the tree pit into it: a cigarette butt, tiny rocks, and paper. He told us that before he conducts a school workshop he first cleans the tree pit and removes objects so the kids don't see anything upsetting (such as condoms) or get turned off by running into dog feces.

Eric took the cultivator and raked and broke up the soil down to about 2 inches. The soil was completely compacted, and he emphasized that the tree roots just below the soil surface need oxygen and that, by loosening the soil, we were helping it get oxygen. He showed us the fine, feathery tree roots that had come above the soil and told us to protect them. Eric took the dandelion weeder and, pushing straight down into the soil, turned the weeder to make holes in the soil to aerate it. He opened a large bag of humus and said that in a normal-sized 5-foot by 5-foot tree pit, he would use a 25-pound bag of humus. He put about half of the humus in the tree pit. This is called "amending the soil." Humus is soil made of organic matter, which is extremely nutritious for the tree. Then he used the cultivator to mix the humus in with the compacted soil. Next came the bag of mulch, which he poured on top of the mixed humus so that it was level with the sidewalk. Mulch protects the soil by helping it retain water and stopping erosion and the growth of weeds. The mulch was moist and red and made the tree bed look so much better and cared for. He warned us not to put the humus and mulch up against the tree. "Leave about an inch around the tree trunk," he said.

I worked on my tree pit with Trudy, the illustrator of this book, for about 45 minutes. After a few minutes of work, a child who lived in the apartment house behind the tree sat down and began to help cultivate the soil. He talked as he worked, using the terminology we all were learning: "cultivate, aerate, mulch." Then we poured water into a bucket with holes as it sat in the tree pit and we watched as the water slowly drained out. As we left, we looked back and thought how much better that spot looked and hoped that it would fare well. Such a simple thing: pick up trash from the tree pit; dig down a couple of inches; make holes in the soil; mix in the humus and water, and then cover everything with mulch. Cultivating, aerating, amending the soil, mulching, and watering make for happy, healthy trees, and happy, healthy trees make for a happy, healthy neighborhood in which to live and work.

HERE ARE FIVE KEY TIPS FOR GOOD TREE CARE:

1. Wear gloves to pick up litter that's in your tree's bed.
2. Aerate soil using a cultivator. Dig down a couple of inches, loosening the soil and pull out weeds. Be careful of tree roots that may be sticking out of the soil.
3. Add a layer of humus or compost material over the newly cultivated soil and mix it in.

4. Add a layer of wood chip mulch over the compost-soil mix. Never put wood chips and compost up against the trunk. There should be one inch around the base of the trunk where there is no compost or mulch.

Proper cultivation of the soil keeps the roots healthy and the tree alive

5. And the most important tip of all! *Water, water, water!* If there hasn't been an inch of rain per week, find a way to bring water to your tree. Water slowly so that most of the water goes into the tree bed. If there are Treegators (watering bags), fill them with water. After a week without rain, a tree would ideally need 15–20 gallons of water.

OTHER WAYS FOR YOU TO HELP TAKE CARE OF TREES:

- Take citizen pruner and tree steward classes. They are free, and you'll take home great tools! Contact Trees New York (treesny.org).
- Get together with your neighbors and build a tree guard.
- Contact Brooklyn Shade (brooklynshade.org) and take a tree guard workshop.
- Visit MillionTreesNYC.org for a tremendous amount of information on planting and caring for urban trees.

Treegators are a great way to keep a tree hydrated during times of drought or low rainfall

Arbor Day Foundation. *What Tree Is That? A Guide to the More Common Trees Found in North America.* Lincoln, NE: Arbor Day Foundation, 2009.

Barnard, Edward Sibley. *New York City Trees: A Field Guide for the Metropolitan Area.* New York: Columbia University Press, 2002.

Brockman, C. Frank, and Rebecca Merrilees. *Trees of North America: A Guide to Field Identification.* Rev. ed. New York: St. Martin's Press, 2002.

Brodie, Christina. *Drawing and Painting Plants.* Portland, OR: Timber Press, 2006.

Choukas-Bradley, Melanie. *City of Trees: The Complete Field Guide to the Trees of Washington, D.C.* 3rd ed. Charlottesville: University of Virginia Press, 2008.

Day, Leslie. *Field Guide to the Natural World of New York City.* Baltimore: Johns Hopkins University Press, 2007.

Glimn-Lacy, Janice, and Peter B. Kaufman. *Botany Illustrated: Introduction to Plants, Major Groups, Flowering Plant Families.* New York: Chapman & Hall, 1984.

Heinrich, Bernd. *The Trees in My Forest.* New York: HarperCollins, 1997.

Hollender, Wendy. *Botanical Drawing: A Beginner's Guide.* New York: Wendy Hollender, 2007.

Ingoglia, Gina. *The Tree Book for Kids and Their Grown Ups.* Brooklyn, NY: Brooklyn Botanic Garden, 2008.

Petrides, George A., and Janet Wehr. *A Field Guide to Eastern Trees: Eastern United States and Canada, Including the Midwest.* Boston: Houghton Mifflin, 1988.

Sibley, David Allen. *The Sibley Guide to Trees.* New York: Alfred Knopf, 2009.

Symonds, George W. D. *The Tree Identification Book.* New York: HarperCollins, 1958.

Tekiela, Stan. *Trees of New York: Field Guide.* Cambridge, MN: Adventure Publications, 2006.

Williams, Michael D. *Identifying Trees: An All-Season Guide to Eastern North America.* Mechanicsburg, PA: Stackpole Books, 2007.

Wunderlich, Eleanor B. *Botanical Illustration in Watercolor.* New York: Watson-Guptill, 1996.

Zomlefer, Wendy B. *Guide to Flowering Plant Families.* Chapel Hill: University of North Carolina Press, 1994.

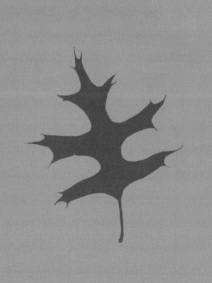

The letter "f" following a page number indicates a figure, "pl" indicates a plate, and "m" indicates a map.